SELLING
HARD LESSONS LEARNED

ALEC BURLAKOFF

SELLING:
HARD LESSONS LEARNED

ALEC BURLAKOFF

Contact:
Training@ABurlakoff.com

ComplianceMitigation.com

Publisher:

Resilient Digital Publishing
32501 Golden Lantern, B-1025
Dana Point, CA 92629

ISBN:

TABLE OF CONTENTS

Forward... 7
1: New York..................................... 9
2: Florida... 25
3: Magnolia Pharmaceuticals.......... 43
4: What's in It for Me?.................... 63
5: Big Pharma.................................. 89
6: Moving to Excelon..................... 103
7: Power and Recognition.............. 119
8: American Scientic...................... 135
9: Ingrid.. 151
10: Mindset at Ingrid..................... 166
11: Collapsing the Wheel............... 185
12: Lessons Learned...................... 203
Epilogue... 219

FORWARD

Alec Burlakoff has a lot of courage. Rather than hiding from bad decisions, he writes openly, hoping to take a meaningful step toward reconciling with society. He shows us our worst decisions do not have to define us. At any time, a person can begin working to make amends and reconcile with society.

In *Selling: Hard Lessons Learned*, Alec takes us on the path that led to his becoming an influential sales leader.

He began his career in the education sector, hoping to make a difference in the lives of at-risk youth. Coaching and mentoring young people brought Alec a sense of fulfillment. Wanting to provide for his growing family, Alec began searching for a more remunerative career.

Given his graduate degree, leaders recognized Alec had the capacity to learn. He stood out as a viable candidate to sell pharmaceuticals. By giving his 100% commitment, Alec trained himself in the vernacular of pharmaceuticals and outperformed his peers. He rose from a sales leader to a leader of sales professionals. During his two-decade career, Alec and his team generated more than $3 billion in revenue for the global pharmaceutical companies he represented.

In this book, Alec shares the principles that worked for him, including:

Focusing attention on what customers wanted rather than what he wanted.

Being disciplined with time management and directing 98% attention on 2% of prospective customers with the highest propensity to advance.

Making 100% commitment to satisfying customers and the profession.

While growing through the ranks, Alec believed his employers wanted him to generate sales by any means necessary. If he brought in more revenue, the employers rewarded his team. They encouraged him to cultivate relationships with doctors that would write prescriptions.

Alec found his niche by looking for "red" doctors—physicians that wanted to earn more.

When Alec began incentivizing doctors to write prescriptions, he violated the law. His role in training others to do the same put him in the crosshairs of government investigations. He lost his family, his livelihood, and he lost his liberty.

Rather than striving to leave the past behind, Alec chose to bare all by writing his story, including all the hard lessons he learned along the way. He

SELLING: HARD LESSONS LEARNED
Alec Burlakoff/ Training@aburlakoff.com

pleaded guilty to a crime and served his federal prison term.

Yet rather than trying to fade into obscurity, he continues taking incremental steps to make amends. By writing his story, Alec invites others to question him and even judge him. He offers insight that sales professionals can use to avoid falling into the morass of bad decisions.

I encourage others to read Alec Burlakoff's work. His books and professional training teach others the hard lessons he learned from a professional sales career. Participants in his courses will also learn how to avoid behavior that can lead to government investigations—and federal prison terms.

For this reason, I highly recommend Alec Burlakoff to leaders who want to teach the principles of ethical sales. He brings meaning to hard lessons and reveals the consequences that follow bad decisions.

Michael Santos
Author of *Earning Freedom: Conquering a 45-Year Prison Term*

CHAPTER 1
LOOKING BACK

What lessons can we learn from failure?

That question has tormented me for the past several years. I'll explain why.

As a young man I anticipated a career in social work, education, or a role in serving others. Then, in my early 20s I lost my way. While working as a guidance counselor at the elite Ridge Pines School in Boca Raton, a snide comment from a wealthy parent felt like a slap in the face. It put me on the path of chasing money.

More than 20 years have passed since then, but the insulting comment still stings. How I responded stings even more, because it reveals a lot about my character at that stage in my life.

In retrospect, I was like many young people, starting my life with aspirations of doing good for society. While studying psychology at Florida State, I got my first job at the Southern Medical Center. I worked with adolescents that struggled with addiction, doing my best to positively influence groups of troubled youth. The job felt fulfilling, even though responsibilities led to my getting punched a few times by some of the more aggressive students.

SELLING: HARD LESSONS LEARNED
Alec Burlakoff/ Training@aburlakoff.com

I could take the abuse and I willingly helped out whenever possible. Later, while working toward my master's degree at Florida International University, I landed a coveted job at the Ridge Pines School, where I anticipated building my career in education.

Everything changed for me on a typical sunny afternoon in Boca Raton. While supervising the parking area where parents retrieved their children after school, I saw a man sitting in his convertible Bentley. He sucked on a huge cigar and blew rings of smoke as if he didn't have a care in the world. As I approached him, reflections from the sparkle of his diamond-faced Rolex blinded me. To comply with the school's no-smoking policy, I asked if he would mind moving off school grounds until he finished the cigar.

He looked me over, as if he were weighing and measuring my worth as a human being. After taking another puff from his cigar, he exhaled in my face. "Petty rules from petty people," he said as he shifted his car into gear and drove away.

That moment changed my dream. As I watched him pull away, rather than feeling a sense of honor at the work I was doing to educate students, I felt like a loser. That was the moment I decided to leave education. I set my sights on finding a career that would lead to more income.

SELLING: HARD LESSONS LEARNED
Alec Burlakoff/ Training@aburlakoff.com

Over the next two decades, I rose to become head of sales for multi-billion-dollar pharmaceutical giants. Reflections on lessons I learned along the way take me back to that moment at the Ridge Pines School, a time when different values defined my life.

As a young man, I measured success through commitment to helping others achieve their highest potential. By grooming young people for leadership, I felt as if I were contributing to society. Sadly, being around so much wealth had a bad influence on me. It gave rise to envy, making me want for what I didn't have.

Education was an honorable profession, but it wasn't going to bring much in the way of income. And without millions in income, others would view me as a loser. Without a strong, inner-moral compass, I felt vulnerable to the perceptions of others. Their opinions of me mattered. I wanted people to see me as being a success.

Those insecurities were rooted in my childhood experiences. Our family groomed me to win—at any cost.

But I didn't win. Bad career decisions led to my losing more than $10 million in personal equity. It led to my being maligned by Jim N. Shastry, the billionaire founder of Ingrid Biologics. Bad decisions led to my name being smeared in the national media. Strangers wrote derisively about me and the

SELLING: HARD LESSONS LEARNED
Alec Burlakoff/ Training@aburlakoff.com

bad choices I made in my leadership role at Ingrid. While working with others to engineer a sales strategy that took the company from startup to billions in revenue, we broke the law.

When Jim Shastry and his team recruited me to lead the sales team at Ingrid, I didn't appreciate the risks. Together, I'm ashamed to admit, we built an aggressive distribution system that contributed to America's opioid epidemic.

With earlier roles in pharmaceutical sales at Magnolia, Stevens and Williams, Excelon, and Argos Bioscience, I focused on one thing: winning at all costs. As a sales professional, I thought about achieving financial results and didn't concern myself with ethical practices.

In retrospect, I see now what was not so clear during my career climb to become a national sales leader in big pharma. When we separate our core values from our business decisions, we start living on the edge. We start walking dangerously close to self-destruction and we expose our employers to regulatory problems—or worse.

Despite growing sales teams that generated more than $1 billion in annual revenues for Ingrid, I failed. I failed to align my values with my goals.

My journey from educator to sales leader offers many lessons. Those who have an interest can learn from these lessons that led to failure, just as they can learn from lessons that led to success.

This book tells the story. The accompanying course work offer suggestions that students, aspiring sales professionals, and corporate executives may consider as they pursue their individual goals. Participants who invest time and energy to master these lessons will reap rewards for a lifetime. Think of the lessons as a self-directed insurance policy, one that should empower participants to make values-based, goal-oriented decisions. Those that learn the lesson well will guard against bad decisions that could eviscerate careers, businesses, and anyone's sense of security.

As the national sales leader for Ingrid Biologics, I had a role in victimizing countless patients and their families. We incentivized doctors to prescribe Stetsine, a fentanyl-based drug that designed for the management of breakthrough pain in cancer patients. In fact, our team encouraged doctors to prescribe Stetsine to any patient that complained of pain. Our corporate policy was wrong, and I knew it was wrong.

Ultimately, my decision to work with the team at Ingrid hurt our community. It hurt my family, contributing to what I have come to call the Burlakoff curse—an affliction that I'll explain in the pages to follow. Through my actions, I became a stain on the honorable profession of pharmaceutical sales.

SELLING: HARD LESSONS LEARNED
Alec Burlakoff/ Training@aburlakoff.com

How did the fall begin?

In coping with the challenges and mental frustrations of a criminal trial, I've learned to ask such questions.

INTROSPECTIONS:

Healing, I think, starts with reflections. To build the future we want, we need to look back. I didn't set out to break laws or violate a code of ethics. In the beginning, I set to work as a school guidance counselor. Yet when I started to allow others to define who or what I was, I started down a bad path.

Still, I had to look back farther. How did I become vulnerable to being so concerned with the ways that others perceived me?

By asking questions of ourselves, we find answers. We learn lessons from how we advanced from one stage in our life to the next. This process of deliberating questions and answering honestly helps us connect the dots. The more time we invest introspecting, the better we prepare ourselves to course correct. Although we may fall off course at any time, we can always adjust. When we reflect on the decisions that led to where we are, and we project where our decisions will lead, we can assess our progress. This critical-thinking strategy makes us more capable of self-directing our way to success.

We are who we are today because of the series of decisions we made yesterday, and the days before. The good news is that at any time, we can start making better decisions. Regardless of where we are, we can start engineering a pathway that will help us navigate the next chapter of our life.

Defining success is a good place to start.

WHAT'S IMPORTANT?

When we define success from the outset, we empower ourselves to chart a course that will help us get there. We can make assessments on whether decisions align with the life we're striving to lead in the months, years, and decades ahead. This lesson can apply to every area of our life, including the careers we build, the business decisions we make, and the relationships we nurture. Our definitions of success reflect our values. Those values become our compass, helping us stay the course so that we grow into the people we want to become.

Conversely, when we fail to define values, we don't have a compass. We become vulnerable to making decisions, with outcomes we did not foresee.

At any time, good questions can help us find our way back. We simply must ask:

- What's the best possible outcome, considering current circumstances?
- What path can we take to get from where we are to where we want to go?
- Do the choices we're making align with the values by which we profess to live?
- How does what we're doing today relate to who we want to become?

I'd like to say that I originated that wisdom of asking good questions. But I didn't.

More than 2,000 years ago, Socrates wrote:

- "The unexamined life is not worth living."

All of us can make better decisions if we train ourselves to examine our choices along the journey. The sooner we start examining our choices, the more likely we are to stay on the pathway to success.

- Who should define success for us?

In truth, we should define our own success. We should not make the mistake of allowing our parents to define our success. Neither our teachers nor our colleagues should define our success. The responsibility is ours to determine all that is important in our life.

I lost my way when I succumbed to the influence of others. Rather than developing my own value system, or inner compass, I turned to others for a definition on what it meant to be successful.

If a total stranger could disrupt my career path, what did it say about my sense of self?

"Petty rules from petty people."

If I had been stronger in my sense of self, in my own definition of success, I would have been indifferent to such a statement. No one else would have power or influence over the decisions that I made. As I look back, I realize that I was happiest when I was working in education, helping young people prepare for successful lives. Instead of pursuing what would lead to my happiness, I allowed someone's insult to shift my focus.

A stranger's statement changed the course of my life, leading me down a dark path that disappointed many.

Lessons on the power of introspection eluded me until my fall into the abyss of despondency.

Once I fell off the edge, reading in philosophy and ethics gave me a toehold. I could begin learning from leaders. From their writings, I grasped what I wish I would have learned much earlier in my life.

Thankfully, it's never too soon—and it's never too late—to start making better decisions.

Besides Socrates, other ancient philosophers inspired me, including Marcus Aurelius, a Roman Emperor. He authored *Meditations* with the singular purpose of guiding his decisions. Although his work has inspired and educated readers for approximately 2,000 years, scholars theorize that he wrote *Meditations* as an exercise in pragmatism. Like an athlete must exercise his body, Marcus Aurelius believed that by writing, he was training his mind to think more critically.

What influence would one decision have on the next?

How did each decision lead to new opportunities, or new threats?

By writing, he could exercise his mind, he could keep himself on track. Marcus Aurelius focused on what mattered most and he made decisions accordingly.

WHO AM I?

In my introspections, I realize how childhood experiences influenced what I eventually became. I didn't live in a household that taught the power of questioning or making deliberate decisions. We learned different lessons.

SELLING: HARD LESSONS LEARNED
Alec Burlakoff/ Training@aburlakoff.com

My name is Alec Burlakoff. On February 8, 1974, a dysfunctional family in New York brought me into the world. We lived on Long Island until I reached adolescence, and then we moved to Florida.

While growing up, I idolized my older brother, Ian. We played sports together and competed with each other. With our dad's influence, we always strove to stand out. My brother was charismatic, like a lightning rod that attracted attention. He discovered weightlifting and began taking steroids as a teenager. I followed in his footsteps, striving to be like him, the biggest most powerful guy in any room. Ian relished the control that he had over me. As we were growing up, I remember him pinning me down for hours at a time, just sitting on my chest so I could not move. He told me that he was doing it for my own good, to make me tougher.

Our parents, Ellyn and Len, were both native New Yorkers. My mom grew up in The Bronx and my dad was from Long Island. Both sides of our parents' families were affluent, but both grandfathers died broke. They were gamblers. My maternal grandfather, Ben, changed his last name from Katz to Kent because anti-Semitism could complicate a business career in those days.

Despite humble beginnings, Grandpa Ben became a successful builder in New York. But his love of gambling undermined his financial security. He entertained my brother and me by picking us from school and taking us to the horse races. Sometimes he'd take us to three race tracks a day.

My grandfather on my father's side, Bernard Burlakoff, a renowned criminal defense attorney, had close ties with organized crime. We grew up around conversations with wise guys, knowing that as a family we were somehow connected. My father bragged about his father's connections with organized crime, and he tried to emulate gangsters. He craved respect, like being recognized when he walked into a restaurant. He always carried a gun. That lifestyle had a huge influence on my brother. Indirectly, it influenced my thinking as well.

By way of extended family, we had aunts and uncles, each of whom became distinguished and financially successful. Most prominent among them is my dad's sister, Sharon. She rose to the highest levels as a corporate lawyer and business executive for one of the largest entertainment companies on the planet. We were not in the same league with our extended family, and in some ways, I think there was a resentment because of the way that our father raised my brother and me.

We were raised to win at all costs. But as I look back, I know that we weren't winners. When we lived in New York, my dad supported our family with a mid-size printing company he owned with a partner. I was young and didn't know too much about the business. It had its ups and downs. We lived in the nicest house, and we didn't want for anything. My dad always drove a new Cadillac, and our parents always sent us away to enjoy an athletic summer camp. But as I recall, there were financial reversals, problems with both banks and the IRS closed my father's business down on several occasions.

Financial pressures, coupled with gambling problems and my dad's gravitational pull to guys associated with organized crime, led to an unhappy childhood. We saw my father being abusive to our mother. Although he was our hero while we were growing up, as I look back, I know that neither moral values nor integrity were too important to my dad. He certainly didn't instill such values in my brother and me. Instead, our dad urged us to do anything necessary to win, whether athletically, in school, or in any course of action we took.

There's a cliché telling us that the apple doesn't fall far from the tree.

Although I love both of my parents dearly, as I look back at my roots, I have more clarity. Reflections on childhood make it clear that life is always a work in progress. Recently, I read an anonymous comment left in response to an article about my role at Ingrid Biologics.

The anonymous reader wrote:

SELLING: HARD LESSONS LEARNED
Alec Burlakoff/ Training@aburlakoff.com

Everyone is a mix of different personal traits, beliefs, and habits. Most of us take all these disparate parts, and somewhere between childhood and becoming an adult, we integrate them into a coherent behavior pattern that is consistent with our core values. Much of what happens after that depends on how sound those values are.

People like Alec Burlakoff are too multifaceted, often charismatic and fun to be around. They say and do the most outrageous things but are usually forgiven. They are unpredictable, which can be exciting and often garners them "Life-of-the-party" status. This can, at first glance, seem charming. They can make you feel like you are the most important person in the room. And for a while, you might be.

The fact is, however, these sorts of people fail miserably at the fundamental task of becoming responsible adults. In failing to harness their ego-centric childhood impulses and establish some sort of adult based behavior code, they may look OK, even better than OK for a while. But they are not.

There is a problem with a life absent of boundaries and a personality not-based upon core principles and beliefs. It leaves one navigating every consequential decision without any guide. There are no guard rails. Most of these people end up smashed to pieces, on the jagged rocks, at the bottom of the cliff they sailed off of when they misjudged a curve. Unfortunately, they seldom drive alone.

Their life stories are often fascinating mixtures of extreme successes and abject failures. Alec Burlakoff's story is not yet complete. That's all I know.

We're all works in progress. And as long as we're willing to introspect, we're capable of writing the next chapter to build the life that we want.

CHAPTER 2:
FLORIDA

By the time I turned 14, New York had run its course for our family. Too young to know the reason behind our parents' decision to uproot our stability, I simply looked forward to the new adventure. Finances, I suspect, influenced the reasons we relocated because we didn't have any friends or family in Florida when we moved.

Previously, I wrote about the ups and downs of my dad's printing business. Owning his own business brought our family the illusion of success. The business employed more than 100 people, and some of the printing presses that people operated looked to be about the size of a small house. In our neighborhood, which was totally blue-collar, others saw us as being prosperous and happy. But I remember our parents fighting all the time. Like many families, they fought about money, or perhaps the want for more money and stability.

Every year, my brother and I went to an athletic camp—an indulgence that others couldn't afford. My dad wanted us to be good in sports and he invested a lot of time training us. He hired private coaches, expecting us to improve faster than other

SELLING: HARD LESSONS LEARNED
Alec Burlakoff/ Training@aburlakoff.com

kids at basketball, baseball, and tennis. We were natural competitors.

My dad sometimes coached our teams, and we were close. As a result of all the extra practice we put in, my brother and I were the most skilled athletes in every sport we played. If he wasn't coaching, our dad was there to cheer us on, expecting us to go all out and win at any cost.

There are many affluent, or even wealthy neighborhoods on Long Island. Kings Park, on the other hand, was a true working-class area. Rather than saying I lived in Kings Park, I told people that I was from Smithtown, the next neighborhood over which was definitely nicer, a grade higher on the status level. For our family, appearances mattered more than good character and honesty, as I'll reveal in the pages ahead. I've learned a lot by thinking about our flaws.

Kings Park, situated on the Western shore, looked across the Long Island Sound toward Fairfield, Connecticut. Mostly Italian families lived around us. They drove old pickup trucks that were filled with tools of their trade and parked them outside their houses. Every weekend brought family drama, and it wasn't uncommon to hear people shouting at each other inside the houses. As far as I knew, we were the only Jews in the area. I considered Kings Park a tough place to grow up.

SELLING: HARD LESSONS LEARNED
Alec Burlakoff/ Training@aburlakoff.com

My brother Ian fit in fine because he was the toughest guy in any room. He was also the biggest weed dealer in high school. As a kid, I remember my friends and me finding a duffle bag filled with his pot. Ian was a born entrepreneur, and as a teenager, he honed his skills by selling weed or running betting pools.

I looked up to Ian, but his recklessness made me feel torn and uneasy. On the one hand, I admired his confidence; on the other hand, I wanted to be a good kid. I didn't want the constant confrontation that my brother thrived on. When our parents told us we were moving to Florida, he was 17.

My dad intended to reinvent himself in Florida, and he trained for a new career as a stockbroker. People liked him. In fact, people that had a surface relationship with my dad would consider him the happiest guy around. They nicknamed him "Giggles" because he always had a smile on his face and people felt better when they were around him. He lived as if on a stage, working hard to provide for our family, though he didn't have any close friends and I perceived him as being anti-social. Outsiders wouldn't know it, but if my dad wasn't working, coaching one of our athletic games, or playing poker, he lay in bed, miserable, struggling with depression.

Despondency, it seems, is part of what I used to call the Burlakoff curse. I learned to break that curse and turn it into the *Burlakoff Success Principle*. But more on that later.

From casual observation, we all looked happy and successful. Yet deep down, during our younger years, we all struggled with inner demons that robbed us of peace and fulfilment. Even my brother, who was insanely talented and gifted in so many ways struggled with depression. Every kid idolized Ian, every girl wanted to be with him. He was a great athlete, super strong, and really smart.

Despite all of his talents and outward charm, Ian battled with what some might construe as mental illnesses. Doctors diagnosed Ian as being bi-polar, and he was on medication. Later, as I learned more about pharmaceuticals, I questioned whether a more complex, dual diagnosis may have been more appropriate. In some settings, he seemed fine and totally in control, while in other settings he could be melancholic, or manic. In any event, being off balance mentally had tragic consequences for my brother.

Everyone in our family seemed susceptible to the Burlakoff curse. We all had to *will* ourselves into a better life. Unfortunately, despite our best efforts, there was always some undercurrent pulling us down. It was a mental conflict that I didn't seem to recognize or grasp until I began investing the time to introspect, to look back and connect the dots. The more I thought about the influences that led me from a small town on Long Island, to build and lead sales teams for billion-dollar pharmaceutical companies, the more I could understand how and why our lives unraveled.

In retrospect, I know that we weren't different from most other families. We all had ups and downs. We all had battles and victories, both in our personal lives and in our careers. Anyone could become successful on surface levels. We could have moments in time where we succeeded financially. Yet if we didn't invest in ourselves, in our mental strength, we'd always be vulnerable to loss.

On the other hand, if we took the time to look back, we could more easily see a different path and how better decisions could've led us to better outcomes.

I regret that I didn't learned such lessons earlier. Life always seems to be characterized by progress, and then resetting. We grow when we look back, when we reflect, when we assess the reasons behind the decisions we make.

When people say *"Hindsight is 20/20,"* they're talking about the power of reflection. We always see more clearly when we look back. Strengthening ourselves requires that we rely upon reflections to make better decisions in the future. It's the reason wise philosophers admonish us to both write and read. By writing and reading we're forced to introspect, to

SELLING: HARD LESSONS LEARNED
Alec Burlakoff/ Training@aburlakoff.com

think about how our decisions today will influence the lives we build and the legacies we leave.

We always have a choice on which path we can take. By taking ownership of our decisions, we empower ourselves, restore confidence, and conquer inner demons that can so easily lead to our demise.

As a young man, my dad earned his business degree from Hofstra University. Despite being good with numbers and finance, he didn't pass the necessary licensing exams to sell securities on the first try. Since time was of the essence, he didn't take the course again and give another try at the test. He needed to get to work and start earning a living.

Relying upon gifts for influencing people, he took a job selling cars for a BMW dealership. He did so well that other dealerships recruited him. After a year, my dad took a position at the Coral Springs auto mall, where he became a legend at a Honda dealership.

While on the job, customers gravitated to my dad. They saw him as being outgoing, smiling, joking, skillful at quickly getting to a common ground with prospects that walked on the lot. He worked many hours, staying at the dealership for as long as it took to reach his goal of selling a car on every shift he worked. At least six months out of every year, my dad won salesman of the month. As a great car salesman, I'd estimate that he earned more than

$200,000 consistently. We weren't rich, but he provided our family with a comfortable life.

If it weren't for his commitment to bail my brother out from debts over the bad bets he had made, my father would be a wealthy man today. Instead, he is old, alone, and broke, very much the same as my grandfather experienced during the winter years of his life.

I don't want that for my life. No one does.

Yet life seems to be filled with patterns. Our parents groom us. If we don't know how to think for ourselves, or make changes, we follow in their footsteps. My grandfathers were both risk takers, always pursuing the adrenaline rush of the next win. One grandfather was a lawyer that worked with high-profile mobsters. Those types of cases brought their own risks. My other grandfather gambled on horses, cards, or anything he could to chase the rush.

As this story will show, I followed in their footsteps through the development of my career. Like both of them, I lost a fortune as a result of decisions I made. We all seemed to share an inability to pause, reflect, and make better decisions. This pattern leads people off a cliff, oblivious to reasons behind the fall. In my grandfathers' case, they were not able to enjoy their senior years. They aged in misery, bringing unhappiness to those they loved and to the people that loved them. In my case, decisions I made brought their own series of complications.

Tragic consequences can happen to any of us, at any time. It's for that reason we must always be sharpening our mindset. Any of us has the power within to carve out our quality of life, our own success, as we define it.

HIGH SCHOOL:

My own battles with depression started to plague me in high school. Up until then, coaches and other kids respected me as a young athlete. Despite being only five-feet-nine-inches tall, I played on the varsity basketball team during my sophomore year. Then I stopped growing while the other kids kept getting taller. Knowing that I wouldn't start on varsity during my junior year, I quit basketball. For the most part, I quit all organized sports even though I likely could have excelled in tennis if I had the self-discipline to stick with the training.

Instead, I followed my brother's footsteps and started injecting steroids. If I wasn't going to grow taller, I decided to excel in other ways. I obsessed over learning everything I could about fitness, nutrition, the best exercises. For my age, I became a savant in the gym and others would come to me for advice on how they could develop more muscular physiques or lose weight.

Lifting weights transformed me, leading to higher levels of confidence. The controversy around steroids didn't matter to me one bit, because it gave me an edge. And as my father taught my brother and me, getting an edge made all the difference in the world. From the vantage point that he taught us, it didn't matter how we won as long as we won. And winning, to my dad, meant getting a better outcome for us, regardless of the cost to others.

In our family, everything was a zero-sum game. For one person to win, another person had to lose. Community wasn't nearly as important as preservation of self. This way of looking at life had tragic consequences for both my brother and me.

After high school, Ian enrolled at Brandeis university, in Massachusetts, where he played on the school's Division III basketball team. He'd always been a star athlete, but his decisions off the court led to problems. When authorities heard that Ian ran the biggest sports book in the university, they launched an investigation.

Fortunately for him, an assistant coach tipped him off just before the school's security force planned to barge through his door and seize evidence. Ian erased everything from his computer. They couldn't bring charges against him, but they kicked him off the team.

Still a good student, Ian graduated in three years. He enrolled in the Marines as a reserve, but while in boot camp, his verbal abuse of a drill sergeant led to Ian's dishonorable discharge and being thrown in the brig. Despite so many talents, Ian couldn't master the mental fortitude of discipline, or the self-restraint necessary to reach his highest potential.

Following college, Ian earned a law degree from Nova Southeastern University. The countless hours he studied to pass the bar didn't matter, because leaders on the court refused to admit Ian into the legal profession. In their view, his multiple arrests for fighting and his dishonorable discharge from the military suggested that my brother lacked the ethical character necessary to practice law. His multiple arrests for fighting, possession of drugs, and a plethora of other problems resulted in his not getting a license to practice law.

Like my father, Ian chose to build his career in auto sales, and he broke all kinds of sales records.

THE TABULA RASA

A philosopher, John Locke, taught that we all come into the world with a blank slate, or a *tabula rasa*, as he called it. We came into the world without knowing anything. As we experienced life, we learned certain behaviors and ways of thinking. Like everyone else, my brother and I learned from what we saw around us. We learned from what we saw in the behavior of our parents and grandparents. They taught us that if we could cheat to get ahead, then we should cheat. This philosophy applied to every area of life.

Sports, for example, should teach us about good character and the importance of a team mentality. But we learned a different lesson. Good character didn't mean nearly as much as winning, by any means necessary. My dad insisted that we play to win, and that we play rough. In basketball, for example, rather than letting another player slide in for an open layup, he expected us to take the player out. If we were coming into a home plate and a catcher could tag us out, our dad expected us to crash into him rather than try to slide into the plate and avoid the tag. If we didn't interrupt the play physically, we wouldn't be riding home with my dad.

He expected us to look for an edge in anything we did. If our family went to an amusement park, like Disney World, my brother and me would shoplift and walk out with all kinds of caps, shirt, or jackets. Rather than scolding us, my dad would laugh, complimenting us on being clever enough to get over. My dad felt proudest when we were getting over on others. Ironically, he didn't see anything wrong with his way of looking at the world. My mom, on the other hand, didn't approve. Silently going along

SELLING: HARD LESSONS LEARNED
Alec Burlakoff/ Training@aburlakoff.com

with what my dad said, thought, or did, was pretty much how she kept the peace in our family.

My dad's view on life became our view. We learned to think like him. Locke wrote that as human beings, all of our behavior is learned from what we experienced, or what we saw in others. We learned how to see the world and how to function in our community. By seeing how others interacted with people and society, we perceived how we should interact.

As I reflect, it wasn't only my father that shaped my way of looking at the world. When my brother and I were children, our grandfather taught us how to cheat at cards. I didn't think anything of keeping an ace hidden when throwing my cards back into a pile. Before leaving to a friend's house to play Monopoly, I'd grab a few hundred-dollar-bills from my own game, and slowly slide them into my pile to get an edge when I was playing with my friends. I didn't see anything wrong with such tactics.

Locke's writings taught that we could *"unlearn"* what we had learned previously. First, we need to become aware. We need to connect our actions with our values. Then we become more conscious, we keep our head in the game.

Until I grew older, during those years when I was trying to cope with the fallout of criminal convictions related to my role with Ingrid Biologics, it never occurred to me that there were flaws in my way of thinking. I never would have thought that I should learn how to "think differently."

Ironically, while building my career in the sales profession, rather than seeing anything wrong with my tactics, I perceived every decision as being strategic, methodical, and necessary to win. I never thought about how my way of thinking influenced the lives of others.

Lessons I've learned through introspection have given me a different perspective. Looking back at my life in its entirety helped me realize why, in the past, principles of balance, temperance, or good character were lost on me.

To do better, to break the Burlakoff curse, I had to train myself to think differently.

LESSONS FROM BRUCELLOSIS

During the summer months following my junior year of high school, I returned to the athletic summer camp in Connecticut where I spent each of my youthful summers. As a child, I went to the camp as a participant, but as a teenager I would return as a counselor, which would've been awesome.

Once I got to the camp, I started feeling sick. I didn't know what hit me. Every morning I got sicker. Nausea made me weak and I couldn't hold my food. Vomiting led to weight loss and exhaustion. When I got home, my dad insisted that the sickness was all in my head. He encouraged me to toughen up, to play basketball, to get myself together.

From a very young age, my dad led me to believe that being sick was a sign of weakness. He would never take a day off because he didn't want anyone to see him as being weak. His influence made an impression on me that carried me through life. Like him, I refused to make myself vulnerable by revealing any type of inner turmoil. That way of thinking influenced decisions I made in my developing career as I grew older.

After several weeks, the fever became so bad that my parents had to take me to the emergency room. Doctors assessed my condition and admitted me, saying they had to run tests to figure out what was wrong. Symptoms of body aches, joint aches, chronic fatigue, and vomiting suggested Lyme's disease but blood tests ruled that out. An innovative doctor ran a separate test. Results came back positive for Brucellosis, the first such case in Florida after more than 20 years. Brucellosis, a rare bacterial infection, could take years to get over.

Despite every type of treatment, I couldn't get well. The disease and antibiotics made me so weak that I had to complete my entire senior year of high school on home study. Feeling isolated and depressed, not wanting to go on, I locked myself in my brother's room and put a gun to my head. Recognizing my fragility, my parents finally sent me to see a mental therapist. I wanted to get better, but it took almost an entire year before my strength returned.

In 1992, I graduated from J.P. Taravella High School, in Coral Springs. Good grades led to my enrollment at Florida State University, in Tallahassee. My struggles with depression influenced me to choose psychology as my major area of study. I didn't know what I wanted to do with my life but getting over my depression would be essential, and I hoped psychology could help.

Both of my parents supported the decision to study psychology. Truthfully, I think they wanted me to find a different way of life. My father continued to perform well in auto sales, and my brother had already joined him on the lot. He earned a living selling cars while he advanced through law school. I think both of them wanted something different for me. Regardless of how I would eventually earn a living, I had to get my mind right. Studying psychology seemed like the right path. Besides helping myself, I liked the possibility of learning concepts that could help others.

THE LOVE OF MY LIFE:

During my junior year at Florida State, my mom set me up on a blind date. While working at

SELLING: HARD LESSONS LEARNED
Alec Burlakoff/ Training@aburlakoff.com

a swimwear store, she became friends with Stephanie, a beautiful young co-worker that graduated from our rival high school. Stephanie was two years younger than me, and she also planned to go to Florida State. When my mom heard that we'd be at the same university, she started laying the groundwork for us to meet.

Stephanie and I hit it off from our first date. I brought her to a jai alai event and taught her how to bet on the exciting sport. On our third date, I brought her on a dinner cruise with gaming. While she ate, I excused myself on the pretense that I had to go to the bathroom. Instead, I slipped down to the blackjack table on the lower level to play a quick hand. She had an idea that I was a bit eccentric, raising some red flags for her, but we hit it off from the start. From my junior year going forward, we dated each other exclusively. Right after Stephanie graduated, she made me the happiest man alive by marrying me.

Stephanie and I made our home in Deerfield Beach, just south of Boca Raton. I pursued my master's degree at Florida International University while I also began my career working in education. Stephanie worked as a licensed interior designer for a high-end firm in Miami.

Our combined earnings put us on a pathway toward a stable, middle-class life. I loved my job as a guidance counselor at the Ridge Pines School, which provided us with insurance and solid benefits. When my brother came to visit me, and he saw that I got to spend my day coaching kids, he thought I was the most fortunate guy on earth—even though I earned a fraction of his pay. By then he was earning several hundred thousand a year selling cars, but he didn't have anywhere near the quality of life that we had. Working with kids and coaching them in sports, made me feel good about myself.

Sadly, feeling good about myself wasn't enough.

Stephanie and I were going to have a baby, and I wanted to give them more than an educator's salary would provide. When a rude parent insulted me with his comment about *petty rules from petty people*, I decided to make a change. Rather than sticking with a job that brought us happiness, I started laying the ground work to make some money.

And that is where this story takes a turn.

CHAPTER 3:
MAGNOLIA PHARMACEUTICALS

Henry Ford is famous for having said:

- "The man who thinks he can and the man who thinks he can't are both right. Which one are you?"

We all grow stronger when we believe in ourselves.

When we accept that we have the power within to influence our place in the world, we have a strong mindset. Strengthening our mindset requires work and personal development. The effort helps us become more successful in any endeavor, including building our careers, or getting through struggles.

This lesson on mindset hasn't always come easily to me. It requires mental discipline and fortitude. Building a stronger mindset has been my anecdote to the Burlakoff curse, but I've always had to *will* myself to exercise this discipline.

For example, during my senior year in high school, I had to change my mindset to get through a tough time. When Brucellosis took me down, I wanted to curl up and let my life slip away. At my

SELLING: HARD LESSONS LEARNED
Alec Burlakoff/ Training@aburlakoff.com

lowest point, I contemplated suicide. The only way through the disease would be to take prescribed medications with awful side effects, including nausea, lethargy, weight gain. It's easier to disregard medications when you know that—at least in the short term—the medications will make you feel even worse.

To get over the illness, I had to work on my mindset. I had to see the best possible outcome. And I had to put myself on a regimen to push through the treatment. Although it took a full year of pain and discomfort, eventually I got better.

Strengthening my mindset helped me cope with Brucellosis, and it also influenced my decision to study psychology. I pursued a career in education, social work, or helping others because the "helping" professions made me feel better. Working with young people brought meaning to my life during my early 20s. I could make a difference in the world by teaching, showing others the techniques that I had learned to build a strong mindset.

A strong mindset gives us the courage to change when our circumstances change. When Stephanie and I were preparing for our first child, building financial stability became more important than the joy and happiness I derived from working with students. I didn't know what kind of career I would pursue, but earning a higher income became a priority. I wanted to provide for my family. But in that pursuit, I definitely lost my way, not looking far enough down the road, not seeing the implications of every choice I made.

To help you understand what led to my fall, and the lessons I learned while recovering from that fall, let me tell you how I got started in sales.

SALES: THE HONORABLE PROFESSION

Sales gets a bad rap. They say that people in sales can be pushy. But if you believed you had something special, and you believed what you had could help someone else, wouldn't you have a duty and responsibility to make sure everyone that needed what you had got what you had?

That's the mindset of an honorable and ethical salesperson. I would defend that mindset all day long.

By the time I made the decision to leave my role as a guidance counselor at Ridge Pines, my father and brother were both doing extremely well in auto sales. Neither of them aspired to become car salesmen, but both of them created a high level of financial success. At his peak, my brother earned more than $500,000 a year as the general manager of a large dealership in South Florida. He lived in an exclusive, gated community of Boca Raton, in a multi-million-dollar house. Financial success didn't bring him happiness. Sadly, despite outward appearances, he and my father were two of the most unhappy people I knew.

Although I could have doubled or tripled my earnings by joining them in car sales, neither Stephanie nor I wanted that kind of life. Having grown up with my father's influence, I learned that succeeding in car sales meant manipulating consumers into buying cars.

During my undergraduate years, I earned a few dollars selling cars on the lot with my dad. It never felt like a good fit for me and I wanted to do better. One time I remember Stephanie's father being in an argument with my dad over something trivial. My father-in-law worked as an emergency room physician and I respected his work ethic, his prestige in the community. When my dad said something that my father-in-law didn't like, he said "Don't give me that car salesman bullshit."

I didn't like the way my father-in-law spoke to my dad, but he wasn't alone. People had a distaste for car salesmen. I didn't want that stigma for my life. I had to find a different way to build stability for my family.

In truth, there isn't anything wrong with the profession of sales of any kind. Sales is an honorable profession. There's nothing wrong with delivering an honest service, helping others understand a specific product. Auto sales, like any kind of sales, takes work. We've got to know what we're offering, and we need to know how to help our prospective customers understand how our product can help them. Whether we're selling cars or toothpicks, if we're acting honorably, we should hold our head high.

Unfortunately, I was insecure. As a young man, I didn't want anyone to see me as a car salesman. I thought it was beneath me. But if others maligned an entire profession, and didn't judge people for their character and integrity, why should I have cared about what they thought? By thinking that I was somehow too good to be a car salesman, I revealed my insecurity.

Instead of turning to my dad or brother for advice on career options, I turned to my own network. Over the years of working at Ridge Pines, I developed relationships with many affluent families. In my role as a coach and a guidance counselor, children spent several hours with me. Several parents were grateful for the influence I had on their children.

Such a scenario helped me open a friendship with the Robinson family. Steve Robinson, one of my young students, had some behavioral challenges at Ridge Pines. We worked together with Steve—basically daily—from the time he was in the sixth grade through the eighth grade. He was an incredibly bright student, but he acted out and disrupted his classes. Other teachers wanted to expel him. As I did with many students, I worked with Steve to get through the tough spells.

I got Steve into sports and spent hours alongside him, using computers to explore industrious ways to use his creative intelligence. Steve's dad, Michael, a prominent surgeon in Boca Raton, appreciated the time I took with his son. I visited the family at their home, getting to know Steve's mother and sister as well. Dr. Robinson took an interest in my career. When I said I was looking for new opportunities, Dr. Robinson suggested pharmaceutical sales. He said he could introduce me to his sales representative at Magnolia Pharmaceuticals, the pharmaceutical giant. Perhaps that would lead to an interview.

Pharmaceutical sales had this big, fancy aura about it. It felt as if people could get some of the respect of the medical profession if they worked as a pharmaceutical rep. I liked the idea of working in big pharma. It would erase that insecurity I had. It stung badly when that parent insulted me in his Bentley. In that moment, I knew that I needed to prove that I was better, that I was somebody. As I perceived it at the time, I saw pharmaceutical sales as a potential steppingstone to build respectability.

In reality, after multiple decades and in pharmaceutical sales, and being responsible for generating billions of dollars in revenues, I can tell you that there isn't anything special about pharmaceutical sales. Being a best-in-class salesperson doesn't have anything to do with the product. It has everything to do with a person's confidence, critical-thinking skills, and mindset. A person can work in pharmaceutical sales and be a portrait of mediocrity, while a person that works as a waitress, or even an adult entertainer, can be an incredibly productive and honest sales professional.

It doesn't take the distinction of a university degree, or a specific product to make sales honorable. It takes the person. Sales is all human-to-human interactions, and if a person does it well, in a principled way, that person should hold his or her head high.

But when I started, I wanted the lure of pharmaceutical sales. Somehow, it would make me feel like a professional—as if the job would give me the credibility I craved.

PROFESSIONAL SALES:

Dr. Robinson could open the door for me to get an interview, but that wasn't going to get me the job. I knew that pharmaceutical sales could be just what I needed. There would be the potential of doubling the income I'd been earning. Further, if I

SELLING: HARD LESSONS LEARNED
Alec Burlakoff/ Training@aburlakoff.com

secured a position, I would make Stephanie proud, which would be priceless.

In my mind, working as a pharmaceutical sales representative would differ in fundamental ways from auto sales. I prepared extensively for the interview.

From my father and brother, I learned that car salesman had to be ready to close the sale on the first meeting. Regardless of what the customer said about needing to think about the car, if he left the lot he'd be gone forever. He would go to another car lot where a more experienced salesperson would close the deal. A good car salesperson would stick with the customer for as long as possible, employing tricks that would keep the conversation going, or employing tactics that would give the customer a sense of ownership—like taking a test drive to the house of a customer's friend. A car salesman makes it hard for the customer to walk away.

Pharmaceutical sales, in my mind, would be much more complicated. I knew it was all about building relationships—what I didn't know was *that all sales required us to build relationships on some level.*

But it's true that professional sales differed from the one-call close that is typical of car sales. Rather than connecting immediately, to succeed in pharmaceutical sales, a person had to build an aura of trust and authenticity.

SELLING: HARD LESSONS LEARNED
Alec Burlakoff/ Training@aburlakoff.com

To prepare for my interview with Magnolia, I went to the library and read *The Doctor as Customer* by Dr. Andy Farah. He's a psychiatrist that wrote about the psychology of selling products to physicians. One of the key lines that I remember Dr. Farah's book:

- "A doctor may not always have time to see his best sales rep. But he'll always have time to see his friend."

Instead of deceiving customers, a professional salesperson would invest time and energy to cultivate lasting relationships. I could get behind such a career, and really saw myself in that role. I would to anything to persuade the sales team at Magnolia to hire me.

Besides reading about pharmaceutical sales, and professional sales, I redid my resume, inserting a photograph so the hiring team would become familiar with my face. From research I had done, I understood that all sales centered on human-to-human connection. At that moment, I needed to make the sale of getting hired. The faster I could get a hiring manager to connect with me, to believe in me, the faster I could get started on building a new career that would deliver fulfillment. For a sales professional, it's always crucial to find every edge, no matter how small, to advance possibilities for that

SELLING: HARD LESSONS LEARNED
Alec Burlakoff/ Training@aburlakoff.com

human-to-human connectivity. When we get people to know, like, and trust us, we position ourselves to close deals. I was determined to close a deal with a hiring manager, and there wasn't anything I wouldn't do to get the job.

During my breaks at Ridge Pines, I drove ten minutes to satellite sales offices so that I could bring doughnuts, cakes, bagels, or other snacks. I worked the sales team as if I were rehearsing to work the doctor's offices I intended to visit.

Again, there wasn't anything I wouldn't do to advance my candidacy as a new hire. After a few telephone interviews, and a few face-to-face meetings, I thought I had the job. Yet when the hiring decision came down, the sales team decided on Chuck Taylor, another candidate. Chuck had previous experience in pharmaceutical sales, and he had built relationships with several doctors that I did not have. I had to admit that experience made him a stronger candidate.

News that I didn't get the job really crushed me. But the recruiter liked the efforts I had made to win the team over, and she pledged to keep my resume on file. A few weeks later, I got a call from another Magnolia hiring manager in nearby West Palm Beach. I went through the process again. It led to my first job in pharmaceuticals, as a sales rep for Magnolia in the West Palm Beach area.

Stephanie and I were super excited about this opportunity. I resigned from my position at Ridge Pines and a few weeks later I boarded a flight for Magnolia's Vancouver's headquarters. As a new hire, I went through the mandatory four-week training to start my new career.

Most of the other new hires had an advantage. With backgrounds in biology, pharmacy, or nursing, they seemed better prepared. Prior scientific training gave them an understanding of medications and mechanisms of action, which we had to learn for each drug. I didn't have any such experience. Every day, we would learn new concepts about the medications we'd be selling, and every day instructors would test us. If anyone didn't pass the daily exams, the instructors would send the candidate home and remove him from the program.

I worked exceptionally hard during that training period. Determined to pass, I memorized the package insert for every drug that was on my list to study.

CATEGORIES AND PERSONALITY TYPES:

Following the scientific training, the instructors taught their best practices for selling to doctors. We'd have to master personality types in order to succeed. The instructors wanted us to use the appropriate sales technique for the appropriate doctor, in accordance with his personal type. We should profile our prospective customers as being:

- A driver,
- An analytical thinker,
- An amiable person, or
- An earthy type.

Each category had specific characteristics. For example, doctors we categorized as drivers would be all business. They would not have time to waste with sales representatives or anyone else. Doctors that fit the "driver" personality type would always be on the go, trying to get to the next patient. They earned money from seeing patients, not wasting time with sales reps. We categorized driven doctors with the color code red. Red Doctors.

Analytical thinkers, on the other hand, want to know the science behind every medication. They wanted to see analytical data, and it would be crucial to lead any sales call with a clinical, well-respected white paper. It would have to be a non-biased study, meaning it came from a third party that extolled the benefits of the drug. Those clinical studies that we would give to the doctor to hold in his hands would help us communicate the drug's properties, side effects, and the mechanisms of action. To prepare for meetings with these types of doctors, we should know everything printed on the package insert. These types of doctors would not have any respect for the representative that didn't know how to discuss medications. We categorized analytical doctors with the color code blue. Blue Doctors.

Amiable doctors wanted to be liked. They talked about their family members, their hobbies, their sports. They responded well to reps that showed personal interest. In an effort to build friendships with all of the reps that called on them, the amiable doctors would be inclined to rotate medications they prescribed, so that all of their reps would benefit equally. From a sales professional's perspective, they were the kiss of death because they would waste valuable time. A salesperson may think he's making progress with an amiable doctor, but in truth, an amiable doctor could never make a sales rep a top earner. Amiable doctors want to be fair, spreading their orders around with every rep that calls on him. We categorized amiable doctors with the color code yellow. Yellow Doctors.

Earthy doctors tended to be very liberal, interested in politics, humanity, and the making of a better world. They valued environmentalism, recycling, and taking care of the planet. We categorized earthy doctors with the color code green. Green Doctors.

If we were going to succeed as sales reps, the instructors taught us, we would have to know our doctors. We would have to learn how to communicate with them on their terms. We had to master the art of making personal connections.

On my own, I quickly understood that I wanted to be the top sales professional in the company. To reach that goal, I would laser my time on Red Doctors. If I could get their time, interest, and attention, I would invest everything I could to become their best friend. I needed to find their WIFM, their *what's in it for me*. By understanding them better, I could become their dedicated business partner, understanding their goals and aspirations.

It was a rash decision and a big risk to put all my concentration on Red Doctors. But bold decisions and being decisive are key components of being a top sales professional. A person needs the strongest critical thinking skills, understanding both threats against time and understanding how to seize opportunities that will maximize time.

During the training in Vancouver, we took our own personality tests. Results from my test came back as being mostly red with a tinge of blue. I would study to learn about the drugs' properties and their mechanisms of action so that I could communicate with the doctors I saw. Ultimately, I wanted to talk business and help the physicians I saw make more money.

From that perspective, becoming the doctor's best friend would become my top priority. If I could become a doctor's best friend, understanding his WIFM, that would lead me to becoming the top sales rep in the country. On the other hand, if I obsessed on being the top sales rep, rather than a doctor's best friend, I would never rise beyond the level of mediocrity.

The client would always come first. I had to find and create ways to integrate my personal life and business life, making myself available any time of the day or night, any day of the week. My wife would become integral to my plan, my partner. Together, we would build our social life around the Red Doctors with whom I intended to cultivate relationships.

Some may view this mindset as being too calculating. But as the legendary philosophers that sidelined as musicians sang:

- It's a long way to the top if you want to rock and roll. (AC/DC)

This concept of understanding personality types helped me immensely in sales, and it can help anyone that wants to reach the top level of the profession. Whether a person is selling sneakers or airplanes, put the customer first.

SELLING: HARD LESSONS LEARNED
Alec Burlakoff/ Training@aburlakoff.com

When I concluded my training in Vancouver, I returned home to proceed through four additional weeks of on-the-job training. I got a new Ford Taurus, a computer, some drug samples, and an expense account. I received a base salary from Magnolia of $80k a year, which was more than 50% higher than what I'd been earning at Ridge Pines. Further, if I performed well, I could earn another $30,000 in performance-based commissions.

This new career, I could sense, was about to become my entire life.

The computer Magnolia provided included a program that gave me access to all of the doctors in my area. I could research their prescription habits, determine how to approach them, and when to approach them.

Being a pharmaceutical sales representative required entrepreneurial thinking. We would sink or swim based on our own ingenuity and our ability to read the market. All reps had the same resources, but we wouldn't all get the same value out of the resources we were given.

Success is a product of our work ethic and critical-thinking skills. Each salesperson that began with my cohort could choose how he or she wanted to attack the market. Our mindset would determine how far we would go. I knew that I wanted to thrive

SELLING: HARD LESSONS LEARNED
Alec Burlakoff/ Training@aburlakoff.com

in the new role. I wanted Stephanie to feel proud of me, and I wanted to provide for her.

To reach the highest level, I knew that I would have to internalize that message I learned when I read the book about how to sell to doctors. They're busy people. They may not want to see a sales rep. But doctors would always have time to see their friends.

I had to learn more about my doctors. I didn't only need to know about their personality types. I needed to learn how to make personal connections with them. What could I do to make more doctors think of me as their best friend?

That was an essential question I had to answer. If I knew how to answer that question, I believed that higher pharmaceutical sales would follow. I'd hit my bonus. I'd make Stephanie proud.

In time, I knew that doctors would see me as a true confident. We'd develop a genuinely close relationship. The relationship may have begun as a strategic effort to provide value, but the more I invested of myself, the closer we would become. They called upon me as a friend would call upon a confidant, and I did the same with them. They would see that I showed a 100 percent commitment and dedication to their needs. They could count on my phone to be my side, ready to respond to their call, their text, or their email any time of day.

SELLING: HARD LESSONS LEARNED
Alec Burlakoff/ Training@aburlakoff.com

In retrospect, I know that I should have asked more questions. I should have considered whether the decisions I was making along the way were consistent with long-term success, or short-term success. I should have been more methodical on the journey.

Those are the lessons we learn over time. Now it's my role to teach them to others, which is why I put together my course on *Burlakoff Success Principles*. Principles, not gimmicks, lead to the highest levels of success.

Ancient philosophers like Marcus Aurelius understood this concept. We're all vulnerable to losing our way. When we contemplate values, mindset, goals, we build defense mechanisms against bad decisions. For that reason, more than 2,000 years ago, Marcus Aurelius wrote *Meditations*. The wisdom is just as relevant today. He wrote out his thoughts in order to keep an internal dialogue going. That inner dialogue kept him on the right path. It became his driving force, giving him confidence and trust that he was making good decisions.

The right decisions were those that would lead to success in months, years, and decades ahead. Instead of chasing short-term victories and wins, we should always consider whether the decisions we're making today will lead to the success we want to achieve later.

SELLING: HARD LESSONS LEARNED
Alec Burlakoff/ Training@aburlakoff.com

Wanting to come out of the gate running, I spent my first month researching all of the doctors I could call upon in my district. I laid out a daily route, and aggressively went out to introduce myself. I learned the power of persistence, breaking down barriers and getting the appointments necessary to open new accounts. Within two months, I could see that I was on a pathway to the top.

Magnolia Pharmaceuticals published a weekly spreadsheet that ranked the top 500 salespeople across the country. Obviously, when I got hired, I didn't have any customers and my name didn't appear on the list. Quickly, I began to rise in those rankings. Each physician I brought into my network led to new prescriptions.

As new hires, we all had the same resources. In fact, other new hires may have thought they had *more* resources because they had the benefit of a scientific background. What they lacked, however, was a full understanding of the WIFM concept:

- What's In It For Me?

I learned the WIFM concept from my father. In fact, the only thing he cared about was whether he had an edge over others. It was the root of every decision he made. By understanding the WIFM concept, I could succeed in sales. To build lasting

SELLING: HARD LESSONS LEARNED
Alec Burlakoff/ Training@aburlakoff.com

relationships with physicians, instead of thinking about my own needs, I put myself in the doctor's seat. By figuring out everything he wanted, I could get everything I wanted.

CHAPTER 4:
WHAT'S IN IT FOR ME?

If we're going to succeed in professional sales, we've got to understand our prospective customers. They're busy. They don't have time to waste with small talk.

I built my career in pharmaceuticals, but the lessons I learned apply to any type of sales. Universally, in sales we have to build relationships first!

In my course, *Burlakoff Success Principles*, I emphasize how hard I worked to make sure that my clients—the doctors I called upon—saw me as *anything other than a sales rep*. They had to consider me as a person of influence, someone they could know, like, and trust. If I didn't coordinate a methodical plan to build mutual respect, I wasn't doing my job and we'd never be able to work together.

And how did I build mutual respect? I listened to what mattered to them and I gave them all the attention in the world.

Mutually beneficial relationships are at the heart of any professional sales career. If relationships fail to profit both the customer and the sales professional, they don't last.

SELLING: HARD LESSONS LEARNED
Alec Burlakoff/ Training@aburlakoff.com

When I began my career in pharmaceutical sales, I understood the opportunity. I had an opportunity to serve others and to build lifelong friendships. If I succeeded as a professional, those relationships would lift my career from mediocrity to prosperity. But not all relationships would succeed. I had to embrace both the failures and the successes, knowing that they were all a part of the journey.

EMBRACING REJECTION:

If I called upon 100 doctors, I might only identify two as viable targets. Missing out on the other 98 was part of the job. No big deal. In fact, I could celebrate those misses. There wasn't any point in complaining that 98% of the doctors I called upon didn't want to do business. I embraced the reality and moved on to the next target. They saved me from wasting time.

Selling felt like going fishing every day. While fishing, I had to choose where I wanted to cast my line. That's targeting! If I were going to select a pond where I'd fish, I wanted to fish in the pond that would give me the best chance of landing the most fish possible, and the biggest fish. I fished for Red doctors. They deserved all of my attention because I knew that one *pure* Red doctor could be worth dozens of Yellow, Green, or even Blue doctors.

Red doctors thought about growing their practices. They wanted to be successful, but always felt as if they could improve. If I could help them reach their goals, I'd become more valuable to them. In turn, they'd become more valuable to me. They were my proverbial needle in the haystack, and I'd search all day to find them. Once I found them, I'd be relentless in cultivating the relationship. I was obsessed with adding value to them.

ADDING VALUE:

But what does it mean *to add value?* Adding value doesn't mean teaching doctors how to practice medicine. That would be absurd. I didn't attend medical school and I am not a doctor. The doctors were the experts in medicine. Still, there were other avenues in which where I could add value. After all, I was an expert in my own domain. I developed expertise from interacting with different practices every day. By giving those lessons to others freely, we'd build upon mutual respect that feeds all great relationships.

Generally speaking, people have enormous respect for the medical profession. With so much deference coming their way, some doctors develop enormous egos. Rather than being intimidated by a big ego, a good sales professional knows how to feed the doctor's ego while simultaneously *building a mutual respect.*

When the client sees the sales professional as a business advisor or partner, the sales professional changes the power dynamic. It enables him to discover the client's WIFM, and to deliver in ways that no one else can, bringing value with every interaction.

TIME MANAGEMENT AND TARGETING:

Economic theorists wrote about the 80/20 rule, emphasizing the importance of prioritizing our time. From my perspective, I could see that 20 percent of my targeted audience would bring me 80 percent of my results. Every professional salesperson had to prioritize time and energy. We had to create more opportunities to invest energy in endeavors that stood the best chance of yielding results.

Magnolia provided lists that included 100s of prospective doctors to call upon. If I devoted the same amount of time and energy to each of them, I'd never rise beyond mediocrity. Why? Because only a small percentage of those doctors would have interest in taking advantage of the value propositions that I could offer.

SELLING: HARD LESSONS LEARNED
Alec Burlakoff/ Training@aburlakoff.com

I knew that I could bring enormous value by targeting the right doctor. To prove themselves as Red Doctors, they'd have to show their willingness to listen, that they'd be accessible to me, and that they had an interest in learning from what I had to offer. Without their time, access, or interest, there would never be an opportunity to build a mutually beneficial relationship.

The Burlakoff Success Principles teaches that in sales—and in life—targeting is essential. If we don't have an effective targeting strategy, we fish in the wrong ponds. To target appropriate clients, we must know what they look like. What are their interests? What drives them? Go a mile deep to understand their interests and you'll develop a client for life.

Without a coherent plan to cultivate relationships with Red Doctors, I could've never become the top salesperson in my industry.

Anyone developing a sales career must know how to target. Targeting is critical. Surround yourself with the right people, with people that provide time, access, and interest in all that you're offering. It's how we choose friends, it's how we choose our partners, and it's how we reach the top of our game.

The 80/20 rule tells us that only 20 out of the 100 doctors I approached would have interest. Burlakoff Success Principles tells us it's more like a 98/2 rule. If I could build relationships with the right 2 percent of doctors, I could get better results than if I were to focus my energy on the other 98 percent of doctors. Rising to the highest level of my profession required me to read doctors efficiently. I had to assess which ones would be most inclined to grow with me.

There truly was no margin for error. Spending too much time with the wrong doctor could literally cost me everything. For that reason, if it wasn't a good fit, as a professional salesperson, I knew that it was time for me to move on. I'd say goodbye. I'd say thank you. And then I'd walk out the door with a smile on my face, happy to avoid wasting time with someone that could never be my partner.

Amateurs mistakenly think *they're* the focal point of the sale. They want to get in front of as many doctors as possible to "teach" about features and benefits, about clinical trials and case studies. Although important, that type of information wouldn't move the needle for a Red doctor.

Doctors won't "learn" from a sales rep. Any pharmaceutical sales rep that fancied himself equal to the doctor's knowledge of science would be a fool.

Professional salespeople develop confidence and expertise in their own niche. They know how to show respect to the doctor's area of expertise. Simultaneously, they know how to communicate expertise in ways that garner respect from the doctor. Success is all about developing that *mutual respect,* a mutually beneficial relationship. With mutual respect, the collaborative partnership flourishes.

Start with an understanding of the market. Busy physicians could earn several thousand dollars per hour by operating efficient practices. They don't want to waste a single minute. For that reason, they tasked all office staff to serve as gatekeepers, keeping people away if those people threaten to interfere with generating revenues.

For that reason, I approached a new doctor's office strategically. I didn't flash my name tag and offer my business card to the receptionist. I'd never open by saying I wanted to speak with the doctor about selling our newest medications. That failed approach would communicate that I'm all about me. Instead, I needed to communicate that I was all about my client. For that reason, I'd tell the receptionist I had *specific ancillary opportunities* that I wanted to present to the doctor.

Any business-minded Red doctor would want to hear about an ancillary opportunity. For him, opportunities sounded like code words. It translated into more success—which was the driver for a true Red Doctor. They didn't only want to make more money, they wanted to be more efficient, more effective with their patients. If I could get in front of a Red doctor, an opportunity opened for us to do business. I'd use every tool at my disposal to cultivate those relationships.

Equally important, if the "ancillary opportunity" didn't grab the doctor's attention, I'd get crucial information:

- He wasn't a true Red Doctor!

That's a crucial piece of data. It convinced me that I needed to move on, to cross him off my list. I'd consider a "No" as a successful interaction, a targeting exercise that helped me move on to the next candidate. There's always a key takeaway and a successful outcome when we accept that targeting is part of our job in sales.

DEVELOPING THE RED DOCTOR:

Once I found a pure Red doctor, I went all in, giving him and his staff all of my attention. I understood that those Red doctors would bring better results. Greens and Yellows would waste my time, the kiss of death to any professional sales career. A Blue Doctor could be okay, but if there's wasn't a mutual respect, or mutually aligned interest, it would be a round peg in a square hole. The relationship would never work. On the other hand, when I found a Red Doctor, both of us knew immediately that we found the right fit. I'd go all in, not only for the doctor, but for the doctor's entire team.

For example, I didn't think twice about hosting pizza parties for the entire office. I'd show up to the office on Tuesdays with 30 pizzas, encouraging staff members to take a box of pizza home with them for their family.

What did I accomplish with such a strategy? A lot!

As a result of my being kind to the staff members, they didn't see me as Alec, the annoying pharmaceutical rep for Magnolia that wasted the doctor's time. Staff members saw me as a friend of the practice. They were more inclined to wave me back. I'd get the keys to the passageway. Or I'd get the inside scope on when would be the best time to show up.

What was in it for the team? They got something they appreciated on their terms: dinner for their families. I served their interests at the right time, providing real value for them.

Any rep could drop off treats to gain favor or attention. But it's crucial to put thought into what we're doing. We've got to think about needs of the targeted audience. What works well for a receptionist doesn't work well for a highly paid and cultivated professional. A receptionist may work for low wages, trading time for money. By bringing pizzas that she could share with her family, we're easing her life. Bingo! We've satisfied her, showing that we care about what's important to her. We understood her WIFM. As a result, we built a mutually aligned relationship. She'd be more inclined to help me because she could see that I was out to help her. It's strategic, deliberate, and focused on mutual success.

CHILDREN AND PETS AND HOBBIES:

When I did have time with the doctor, I kept my eyes open, looking for clues. If I saw photographs of the doctor proudly holding a large fish that he landed, I took that into my calculus. I tried to book a t-time for the doctor if I saw golf clubs. If I saw pictures of the doctor at an athletic event with his children, I took that information in.

Once I saw a photograph with a doctor cheering on his son's little league team. Immediately, I saw an opportunity. I told him that I was trying to interest my daughter in baseball. I asked if it would be alright if I brought my daughter to a game so we could watch his son play. The doctor became one of my best friends.

Regardless of what type of sales we're in, it's crucial that we always remember we're working with human beings. We need to create that connection. All human beings have close feelings for their children and their pets. Kids and pets are people's priority. When we focus on those two priorities, we can be sure that we're getting closer to our targeted clients. We're showing concern for aspects of life that are important to them. That's the key that will lead us to success in sales—and in life.

All personal details could give me an edge. The more I knew about the doctor, the more resources I had to cultivate a relationship.

On a more Machiavellian note, personal details can also give us an edge, or leverage. Remember, business is real. Some say business is like war. It could get ugly at any time. When we develop leverage, we get tools to keep power equally divided—we built that mutual respect. We want to provide intimate details about our life. In turn we want to get intimate details. Give and get!

For example, I may have a relationship with a married physician. He may like strippers. He may have a girlfriend on the side. No judgment. That's life. The more I know about him, the more leverage I have. I wouldn't want to use that leverage in a bad way. But in a pinch, I wouldn't hesitate to apply pressure in order to keep our business relationship on track. I want valuable tools, leverage that I can apply to keep the business going. To give, I've got to get!

SELLING: HARD LESSONS LEARNED
Alec Burlakoff/ Training@aburlakoff.com

OPPORTUNITIES:

With lower-end sales, people felt compelled to close the sale as quickly as possible, but always on the first meeting. They didn't have time to work on building or developing the relationship. In professional sales, on the other hand, taking the time to develop the relationship makes all the difference in the world.

MUTUAL AFFINITY AND RESPECT:

What do I mean when I say it's important to become the "best friend?" It's not a drinking buddy. It's not someone we slap on the back and ask "how's it going?" When I taught other sales people how to become best-in-class, I frequently encouraged them to "be the doctor's best friend." Surprisingly, few understood my meaning.

Being someone's best friend was a metaphor for developing mutual affinity and respect. Ideally, we want to cultivate the kind of affinity that a doctor feels when he invites someone to his wedding, to his son's bar mitzvah, to his daughter's birthday party. It's a real relationship that each party can count upon.

Closing the sale didn't mean getting the doctor to write a prescription. We needed to cultivate a level of trust that would help him rely upon us for strategies to build a more profitable practice. By helping him succeed, the doctor would learn to count on us in the same way that he counts on a friend.

Once I built that trust with a doctor, I could talk with him about business. I would say, "Doctor, listen. You and I both know you're in the business of healing. You make people feel better. You give people inspiration to move on with their lives. When they come to you, they're weak, either with psychological problems or they're in pain. They're coming to you out of faith."

The doctor listens, nods, appreciates that I understand the challenges of his practice. He respects the advice I'm about to offer, recognizing that I'm an expert in my domain in the same way that he is an expert in his domain.

"I know you're a great doctor. Every time I come in here, your waiting room is full. You've got to make those patients feel better as quickly as possible. The clock is ticking before they even sit in your waiting room. You've got to make them feel as if you're providing value. That's what the patient expects, and that's what Magnolia's medications deliver." I'd let that soak in.

"But I don't have to tell you that because you're the expert in medicine, and you know the science. The initial success you provide is like a lead magnet, bringing your patient closer to the next order. Giving him that small dose of the success he

SELLING: HARD LESSONS LEARNED
Alec Burlakoff / Training@aburlakoff.com

wanted makes your patient more receptive to your core offer. He's now more inclined to sign up for the interventional medicine, the surgery, the procedure that you're going to provide next."

When I talk with the doctor about ways that Magnolia's medicine can help his practice grow, I'm building that trust, that credibility. He wants to listen and I give him more to consider. He's soaking it up because I've changed the power dynamic. At that moment, I'm not the sales rep. I'm his business consultant.

"We both know the studies for Magnolia products are best in class. Here's what in it for you. If the patient comes in, and you can see him fast, prescribe the medication and make him feel better quickly, you're a miracle worker. The patient's been suffering for a long time. As a result of seeing you, the patient isn't bed-ridden or depressed any more. He's going to the pool, he's playing canasta, he's playing with his kids, or having sex with his wife. He's got his life back. He's telling his friends how you made him feel better."

The doctor is engaged, getting the message.

"What better way to expand your market? Patients that you've healed become your practice's biggest ambassadors. They start selling you, Doc, as if they're live testimonials, or infomercials on your excellence. By making your patients feel better as quickly as possible, you're not only practicing good medicine, you're practicing good business. That's an area where I can help you immensely."

Could I have that conversation with every doctor? No. But if I've targeted well, I'd have this conversation with a Red Doctor every day. And every day he would feel great about seeing me. He'd know that I'm an expert in my own domain, but also a personal coach, providing value that helps him build a more successful practice.

As I stated earlier, if I called on 100 doctors, 98 of those doctors would be poor targets. They'd refuse to see me. Or we'd only have a cursory relationship. I wouldn't have earned the right to have such a conversation with those doctors. But out of those 100 doctors I called upon, I'd have enormous trust and respect from two of them. Then I'd target those two, giving them all the attention and time, they wanted.

To get to the level of trust where I could have such a conversation, we had to get to the point where we were close, understanding each other. I'd spend time with him on his terms, where he would be most comfortable, where he'd let his guard down. We would have gone fishing together. We would have played golf together. We would have bonded together in ways that best suited the doctor.

SELLING: HARD LESSONS LEARNED
Alec Burlakoff/ Training@aburlakoff.com

It didn't matter what he liked. If the doctor liked women, I'd treat him to a strip club, or a visit to a massage parlor. It was business at the highest level, bringing value with every meeting. The closer I got to him, the more I could understand his interests. And if I understood his interests, I could satisfy the "what's-in-it-for-me" question. It's all part of the slow, methodical, deliberate pursuit of leverage. The more I understood about my targeted Red Doctor, the better I could serve him and make him more successful.

I didn't want to waste the doctor's time during office hours. Office time was about economics. He had an overhead and he needed to generate revenues, not listen to pitches from a rep. It was my responsibility to know and understand his practice, to make it more successful. If I tried to see him when it was easiest for me, I could never bring him value. The idea of a 9 to 5 job for a sales professional is absurd. If we want to be best in class, we work on our client's watch, not ours.

Our conversations took place off site, in accordance with the doctor's interest. But during those conversations, I'd always look for opportunities to bring it back to making the doctor more successful. The more I understood about him and his practice, the more value I could provide. If he didn't see me as adding value, he'd see me as a nuisance and avoid me. We had to develop that mutual respect and trust.

KEY OPINION LEADERS:

At the start of every relationship, the doctor was in power. His time was valuable. If he considered a sales rep a waste of his time, he wouldn't listen. But if the doctor saw opportunities to earn more through his relationship with the sales rep, everything changed, including the power dynamic.

Any rep that could understand his customer's *what's-in-it-for-me* question could always become more powerful. He could become more influential, changing the power dynamic. A sales professional differentiates himself from a salesman by building that mutual respect with the customers he serves.

Once I developed a strong relationship with a Red doctor, I learned that I could use the Key Opinion Leader program to convert the doctor into a brand ambassador for Magnolia. By developing Key Opinion Leaders, I changed the power dynamic between my doctors and me, even though I'd only been a sales rep for a couple of months. I found this Key Opinion Leader program to be very effective and popular with physicians. It played to their ego, and as I wrote earlier, ego is common with anyone in a position of power. Never be intimidated by big ego. Feed the ego, use the ego to change the power dynamic.

Magnolia understood that doctors would want to learn about medications from other doctors. When a doctor truly believed in the ways that a medication benefitted patients, that doctor could champion the drug, offering powerful endorsements.

To encourage doctors to become Key Opinion Leaders, or KOLs, Magnolia authorized me to offer honorarium payments. Depending upon the doctor's credentials, he could earn $1,500 to $3,000 for each presentation he made on a specific medication. Perhaps equally as important as the money would be the trust and respect that he'd build by becoming a KOL.

Since I sold Pristor and Atipal for Magnolia Pharmaceuticals, once I developed really strong relationships with my doctors, I invited them to become KOLs for those two drugs. We'd provide the doctors with PowerPoint slides and literature that featured all of the clinical data. The doctors followed those slides verbatim. At the end of the presentation, during the question and answer session, they could speak openly and freely, talking about their own clinical experience and what they saw in their patients that used Pristor or Atipal.

I'd invite a dozen doctors to attend a private dinner at a high-end restaurant. After listening to my Key Opinion Leader rave about the benefits of Pristor or Atipal, those other doctors would begin writing more prescriptions too. All of those prescriptions would be credited to my account.

The doctors would count on that honorarium income, as well as the trust and respect they got from being recognized by their peers. It brought me an intangible leverage.

By cultivating relationships with Red doctors, and understanding what they wanted from the relationship, I could get what I wanted from the relationship. That would not have been possible if we were not colleagues, on the same level.

CLIMBING THE RANKS:

Other sales reps got the same reports from Magnolia that I was getting. Each week, I jumped higher in the top-sales-rep rankings. My quarterly bonuses were maxing out, with lump-sum checks for $24,000. Whenever I encountered other reps at training sessions, seminars, or conventions, they'd compliment me on how well I was doing. Then they'd ask for advice, wondering what they could do to accelerate their sales.

"It was simple," I told them. "I have an awesome Key Opinion Leader. Every time I coordinate a dinner with other doctors, he champions the drug, showing the medication's benefits in ways the other doctors understand. Every doctor that hears him speak starts writing more prescriptions. You should schedule him to speak at your dinners."

By opening more opportunities for my KOL to speak, what was I doing? I was adding value! I was strengthening my level of influence with the doctor.

In every meeting, I had an agenda. It was all business, every discussion. If there was an opportunity to develop my career, there wouldn't be any value in the interaction. That's the mark of a sales professional. Developing business relationships and transactions was how I created value, and it was my number 1 agenda.

When other sales reps began inviting my Red doctors to present at dinners they coordinated, I got more leverage. Although I helped the other sales reps earn more commissions, my KOLs earned more. By presenting at several dinners each week, my Red doctors could supplement their income by $30,000 to $40,000 in honorariums per month. They loved it. And the sales reps loved it, too, because suddenly they were getting more doctors to write prescriptions for them.

Simultaneously, my influence was growing all around. My name started to ring bells. Although I was only in my first year as a pharmaceutical rep for Magnolia, I was building influence at all levels, opening new opportunities every day.

The KOL program felt like an experiment with Pavlov's law. The doctor would give a presentation, and a few days later he'd get the reward. Or they'd get a compliment on their presentation from a colleague. It got to the point where doctors would ask me to coordinate more speaking events for them. I had leverage.

"I can help you get more honorariums, doc. But you've got to write more scripts. Other doctors are writing more prescriptions, so they're in line to get those honorariums. If you wrote more prescriptions, I could steer more speaking opportunities your way."

Using leverage!

The doctor might object, saying that he had a small practice and he couldn't write more prescriptions. Yet since I developed a strong relationship with him, I was in a position of strength. I could help him close more business, even if the doctor's small practice saw only five patients a day, he could easily write one prescription a day. After all, every patient that came to see him was a candidate for medications Magnolia offered. By writing one prescription a day, a single Red doctor could make me the top pharmaceutical rep in my district.

If I didn't take the time to cultivate a friendship with my doctor, I wouldn't be able to make such a pitch. I wouldn't have "earned the right" to speak with him that way. In fact, making such a presentation to the wrong doctor would result in offending the doctor. He'd consider me acting outside of my

SELLING: HARD LESSONS LEARNED
Alec Burlakoff/ Training@aburlakoff.com

scope, and he might call my manager. Or worse, he might report me to authorities for being too aggressive. People think it's easy to offer value and get a great return on investment. In truth, it's an accomplishment few professionals ever achieve.

Yet I changed the dynamic. I became the KOL, and the doctor looked to me for guidance. As a result of the attention I steered his way, the doctor became more successful, and he appreciated what I could do for him. I wasn't the sales rep. I was his friend, his consultant, his business partner. He gladly listened to my advice and gladly wrote at least one new prescription each day.

By cultivating great relationships with two Red doctors, I won the Fast Start award at Magnolia. I won the PEER award, with all of the others from my cohort of new hires agreeing that I was the most inspiring new rep. As a result of my high sales volume, I won an all-expenses paid trip to a top-of-the-line resort in Puerto Rico for my wife and me. At nine months, Magnolia's vice president of sales awarded me with the Rookie of the Year Award.

A couple of days later, Magnolia fired me. I became a victim of my own success.

THE ROLLOUT:

Magnolia had successfully used a rollout program for a new diabetes drug in the past. Effectively, they created a template that sales reps could follow. By using the template, reps would get their doctors to prescribe samples of the new drug, accelerating sales.

Our division had never used the rollout program in the past. Yet as a result of the successful rollout with the new diabetes drug in another district, our sales leaders wanted to try something similar.

We were in the neuroscience division, and our scientists created a new form of Pristor. Patients would be able to use the new medication once a week rather than once a day. To accelerate distributions of the new drug, our leaders launched the Switch Program. Sales leaders wanted doctors to switch from prescribing the once-a-day Pristor to the new once-a-week Pristor. During one of our sales meetings, our leaders asked how many reps anticipated that they could persuade doctors to participate in the Switch Program.

In medicine, doctors have a general rule. When patients are stable, they don't like to make any changes. For that reason, none of the other sales reps offered to participate in the Switch Program. They didn't have confidence that they could influence their doctors to participate.

SELLING: HARD LESSONS LEARNED
Alec Burlakoff/ Training@aburlakoff.com

But I changed the power dynamic with my doctors. They didn't see me as a rep. They saw me as a consultant, a business partner, a confidant. We were best friends, not in the corny sense that some use the term. We were colleagues, with mutually aligned interests. I didn't have any doubt in the world that they'd participate in anything I suggested. We had a mutual respect, and if I reached out to them, they understood that I was doing something to make them more successful.

Our leaders helped us with the rollout. They designed templates that would remove all of the work for the doctors. It included a letter highlighting the benefits of a once-a-week Pristor medication versus a once-a-day Pristor medication. That letter encouraged patients to stop taking their current anti-depressants and to switch to the new once-a-week Pristor, then to schedule an appointment with the doctor for a follow up. We provided packages the doctors could send with the letter, including sample prescriptions of Pristor.

I spoke with my doctors and introduced the rollout plan, making sure I responded to their what's-in-it-for-me question. Not only would they help their patients, but they'd get new office visits. To accelerate the rollout, I encouraged the doctors to review their records. They should find every patient that was on an anti-depressant. The doctors readily agreed to send each of those patients the letters and sample prescriptions. Doctors sent out rollout packages to thousands of patients in their data base.

Unfortunately, my doctors didn't scrub their database before sending out the rollout packages we put together. Some of the patients that received the free samples were no longer on medication. Some were dead. Some were underage. The rollout led to complaints and an unmitigated public relations disaster for Magnolia.

Although I adhered to the rollout program precisely as superiors advised, and the Health Insurance Portability and Accountable Act (HIPAA) precluded me from having any access to patient records, I was part of a team that was blamed. Although I didn't have any way of reviewing the patients in the doctor's database, Magnolia needed to blame someone. I became one of the scapegoats.

Without warning, my career at Magnolia ended abruptly. I was fired a few days after I won Rookie of the Year for leading the sales charge.

That's life in the big city!

Fortunately, as a sales pro, I was ready to land on my feet.

CHAPTER 5:
BIG PHARMA

My career at Magnolia ended abruptly. Local media published a negative story describing flaws with the new medication rollout. Two days later, I was summoned to a local Marriott for a meeting with leaders from Magnolia's headquarters. Someone had to go and the company determined it would be me. Five minutes into the meeting, leaders directed me to hand over the keys to my company car and computer. They sent me packing.

Following the unexpected derailment of my career plans with Magnolia, I felt disappointed and unsettled. Stephanie had just given birth to our first daughter, Breanna. Without a job, I didn't know how I would provide for our family.

During those nine months with Magnolia, I performed well, learning a great deal about complex sales. By earning Rookie of the Year Award, the Fast Start Award, the Peer to Peer Award, and every bonus possible, I sensed success ahead. Pharmaceutical sales gave me an identity—I'd found my calling. If I were to continue growing in my career, I'd even earn respect from my dad and brother.

SELLING: HARD LESSONS LEARNED
Alec Burlakoff/ Training@aburlakoff.com

Those two were crushing it in auto sales, my brother especially. We were close as a family, but my lower earnings left me feeling as if I never measured up to their success. As the little brother, I didn't have a seat at the table. My job selling pharmaceuticals opened the opportunity for me to grow; I could potentially become more successful than either my brother or my father.

By developing my career in pharmaceutical sales, I felt proud. Rather than mastering the "one-call close," as happens in auto sales, I nurtured relationships with well-educated, sophisticated professionals. At a surface level, people might assume that my high-performance, upward trajectory at Magnolia resulted from my simply "buying" doctors with the promise of honorariums. From my vantage point, that assumption would be an incredibly simplistic way of looking at the complexities of the pharmaceutical sales market.

Pharmaceutical sales reps play a crucial role in healthcare. Society demands constant development of new medications that would improve the quality of life for people. We're not physicians, but we provide fuel that feeds ongoing, innovative R & D. Enormous resources are required when creating those medications. According to Wikipedia, health economists peg the current cost of drug development at $1.7 billion. Without effective sales and marketing, pharmaceutical companies would never recoup those costs. If they couldn't recoup development costs, there wouldn't be any incentive to develop more medications.

After clinical trials and approval from regulatory boards like the Food and Drug Administration, physicians must learn how new medications serve their patients. As sales reps, it's our job to champion the benefits of pharmaceuticals. But getting that message to a busy physician is an enormously heavy lift.

Consider the obstacles. Office staff serve as gate keepers to protect the doctor's time. Other competing sales reps may already have relationships with physicians. They do not want their doctors to start prescribing new medications from any other reps. Further, physicians are reluctant prospects. They invested hundreds of thousands of dollars, or perhaps millions of dollars in education and career development. Physicians are trained to learn from other physicians, not from sales reps with a limited understanding of medications.

Persuading doctors to become champions of pharmaceutical medications helped to grow the industry. I always felt proud of the work that I was doing. By building relationships with more doctors, I played a small role in generating resources to advance science.

SELLING: HARD LESSONS LEARNED
Alec Burlakoff/ Training@aburlakoff.com

Despite challenges of overcoming reluctance and cynicism from doctors, I earned respect from others in the industry. I outperformed each peer in my cohort of new hires. When my superiors at Magnolia tasked me with the new-medication rollout, I did exactly what they told me to do. Yet the company fired me when the coordinated rollout failed to go as anticipated.

RISE OF THE PHOENIX:

Fortunately, my career did not skip a beat. By the end of the week, recruiters from other big-pharma companies contacted me. Alan, a district manager for a Stevens and Williams division asked me to meet with him. As a district manager, Alan oversaw 10 sales reps that were responsible for selling Spurdisel to physicians in Florida. Spurdisel was a specialty drug that psychiatrists prescribed to treat patients they diagnosed with refractory depression, schizophrenia, and bipolar disorders.

As it turns out, being fired by Magnolia opened a new opportunity to advance my career. Lessons learned in leadership and personal development arose from what—at the time—felt like a tremendous personal and professional setback.

Growing in any career, or succeeding in any path, requires that we devote ourselves with a 100% commitment. Once I had an opportunity to interview for my first job as a pharmaceutical sales rep, I applied myself completely. And when I got the job, I studied extensively to learn everything possible about Pristor and Atipal, the two medications I sold for Magnolia. As a result of giving 100% to the effort, I learned how to break down barriers, build relationships, and earn trust from physicians. The industry took note of my success.

Magnolia ostensibly let me go because of the rollout fiasco. In reality, they fired me because of reasons related to corporate politics or public relations. Yet as a result of the commitment I made to excellence while on the job, other leaders in big pharma became aware of me. They wanted me on their team. Alan made me an offer to join Stevens and Williams. Since he represented a specialty drug, I got to call upon psychiatrists rather than general practitioners. The supposed setback from Magnolia turned into a promotion at Stevens and Williams's Stansel Pharmaceuticals division, with even more earning potential.

SEARCHING FOR REDS:

When I joined Stansel, distributions for Spurdisel underperformed against its competitors—Atipal and Loquelsan—in the Boca Raton district. By using the same techniques that had catapulted me to the top of sales for Magnolia, I intended to become the market leader. A top-tier rep would build a business that generated approximately 100 prescriptions from doctors each month. A mediocre rep would only get about 30 prescriptions per month. Psychiatrists in Boca Raton were only writing about 10 prescriptions for Spurdisel each month, so I had a long way to climb.

Immediately, I began calling upon the leading psychiatrists, doing everything possible to identify the top Red Doctors. Since each of those doctors had pre-existing relationships with reps for Loquelsan and Atipal, I faced enormous hurdles in getting through to them. For that reason, I focused all of my attention on the top-three psychiatrists that I could find.

If the ultimate goal was to find and persuade the right psychiatrists to champion the benefits of the drug, what steps would I have to follow to get their attention? That's the question all representatives of a "complex sale" should understand—regardless of *what* they're selling. I'll explain the micro steps that I took as a representative of Spurdisel to get me there.

The first step would be to understand the total available market. How many psychiatrists were in the district?

To answer that question, I researched the database that our company provided. The homework began with research. From that research, I dug deeper and discovered how many prescriptions each psychiatrist wrote. If a psychiatrist wrote a few prescriptions per month of several different medications, I had a data point to consider. If a psychiatrist wrote several prescriptions of a single medication each month, I had another data point to consider.

This simple analysis helped me implement the *Burlakoff Principle of 98/2*. As I described in the previous chapter, it's a variation of the 80/20 rule, also known as the Pareto Principle. I knew that 2 percent of the doctors could get me 98 percent of the results I wanted to achieve. The work began with a search for the right 2 percent.

Yet identifying the 2 percent took extraordinary effort and ingenuity. After all, research would have shown that they wrote several prescriptions each month of a single medication. That means those doctors would be of high value to the reps selling that medication. Somehow, I would need to get through the gatekeeper. Then I would need to open a relationship with an extremely busy psychiatrist. Over time, I would need to find the doctor's "what's-in-it-for-me" question. Then I would need to overcome the doctor's objections and prove worthy of the doctor's trust. Only then could I close the deal. And closing the deal meant making the psychiatrist part of my stable of speakers that would champion Spurdisel.

SELLING: HARD LESSONS LEARNED
Alec Burlakoff/ Training@aburlakoff.com

My plan of becoming the top sales rep for Stansel Pharmaceuticals required me to build a stable of psychiatrists to champion Spurdisel. As I wrote earlier, I knew that doctors preferred to learn from doctors. The long-term vision required that I build my team of speakers. Ideally, I set goals of building a stable of five speakers that I could call upon. I'd want them to be my stars. I'd have another five speakers that I would groom, keeping them ready in the event of an opening in my roster. Again, this was a long-term strategy that would require me to invest my time wisely.

A mediocre salesperson would try to close the deal too soon. I often observed this amateurish approach from my colleagues. Foolishly, they led with an offer to pay the doctor to speak. That myopic approach violated every principle of the professional sale. It's a catastrophic and fatal error in the sales process, equivalent to meeting someone on a blind date and asking for a divorce before the marriage even began.

Professional sales are complex. We don't go for the one-call close. Instead, we court our sophisticated consumers and nurture the relationship, taking every step necessary to earn trust. We do our homework and we show that we're a worthy partner for a long-term relationship.

Through my research, I identified three Red doctors. I could tell they that saw an average of 80 patients each day. I could do the math on that. If the psychiatrist saw 80 patients per day, that meant the doctor saw each patient for a few minutes—enough time for a cursory exam, diagnosis, prescription, and then on to the next patient. This information let me know that I had found my ideal Red doctors. They were all about business, yet they were prescribing Loquelsan rather than Spurdisel. I had to get them to switch.

Before I called upon my prospective Red targets, I learned everything possible about Spurdisel. If physicians were going to ask questions about science or case studies, I had to respond with correct answers and compelling case outcomes. Wanting them to prescribe Spurdisel was one thing. Getting them to make the switch from Loquelsan would require commitment and ingenuity. I could not rush any part of the sales process.

With my master's in social work and therapy, I had a commonality to those mental health professions. But that wouldn't be enough to convince physicians to abandon the sales rep that had been consistently calling upon them. I understood the challenge. In the same way I applied myself at Magnolia, I made a 100 percent commitment to success with Stansel Pharmaceuticals.

SELLING: HARD LESSONS LEARNED
Alec Burlakoff/ Training@aburlakoff.com

COURTING RED:

I set my sights on Dr. John as my first candidate. He had degrees from Ivy League universities and a robust clinical practice. I began calling upon him to introduce myself. He put me to the test, grilling me on results of case studies for Spurdisel. Rather than asking to learn about the medication, he asked questions to probe the depth of my knowledge. Had I gone in there blindly, chances of working with Dr. John would have vanished.

Dr. John showed me a photograph where he was standing beside Jenny, an attractive young woman that represented Loquelsan, Zenith's blockbuster drug. He told me that he had been prescribing Loquelsan for several years. Basically, he told me, Loquelsan and Spurdisel showed similar results. Why should he consider switching when he had a solid relationship with his rep at Zenith?

Dr. John likely appreciated the attention he received from Jenny. What man wouldn't? But to his core, I recognized that he was a pure Red doctor. As a businessman, he wanted to grow. I assured him that I would compete aggressively for his business and that I wouldn't stop trying until he understood my obsession with serving doctors on my team.

Although he considered Loquelsan and Spurdisel as being basically equivalent medications, I had to win him over to my drug. I was 100 percent committed to the challenge. To succeed in my career, I explained, I needed to help him become more successful. In total transparency, I explained that I would earn an income based on the market share I controlled. Either I succeeded in building a relationship with him, or I would be mediocre. And there wasn't anything mediocre about me! I intended to be the best in the world in this role. That meant fighting to make his practice more successful.

What's in it for me? I knew Dr. John had this question in his mind, and I gave him a direct answer. I intended to be his best friend.

That's what it meant to go all in. I needed to win John's trust and let him know that I would be loyal to him to the end. I preferred to have a close relationship with one doctor than have amiable relationships with 100 doctors.

"I'm at the Boca fitness every morning at 5:00 am on the treadmill," he told me. "If you can get the treadmill next to me, you'll get an hour of my time."

Not a problem. I showed up at the gym early enough to reserve two treadmills. And when Dr. John showed up, we both started to exercise. While jogging lightly, we shared conversation. We spoke about the stock market, about real estate values, about tax policies. I showed up every day, always reserving a spot for him. One morning, all of the side-by-side treadmills were taken. Knowing the value of

SELLING: HARD LESSONS LEARNED
Alec Burlakoff/ Training@aburlakoff.com

a conversation with Dr. John, I stood in the middle of the aisle to make an announcement. "I need two side-by-side treadmills. I've got a $50 bill for two people that can make it happen."

Dr. John laughed. "You meant it when you said you'd go all in."

I understood Dr. John's WIFM question. He loved treating patients. Yet in order to earn the income he needed, his practice had become a factory.

"I can help you out." We'd bonded sufficiently and I felt ready to make the offer. "You want to see fewer patients and get back to doing what you love. Become a champion of Spurdisel and I'll keep you busy speaking. You can cut your patient load in half, opening more time for therapy. We'll supplement your income with speaking fees, to make up for revenue you may lose from seeing fewer patients each day."

Jenny arranged for him to speak as much as her budget would allow, he said. Income from speaking fees for Zenith wasn't enough to have a material impact on his bottom line.

Jenny hadn't done her research. Good looks and some luck may have led to her building a relationship with a pure Red doctor. But she missed the key success component. Jenny never learned how to satisfy Dr. John's WIFM question.

SELLING: HARD LESSONS LEARNED
Alec Burlakoff/ Training@aburlakoff.com

A best-in-class sales rep knows the value of asking FOEQ—Focused, Open-ended Questions. Jenny didn't, and as a result, she lost a valuable account. A client that didn't get his WIFM-question answered would be a client that I could steal.

"Dr. John, think of yourself as an athlete. You're a great quarterback playing for the New York Jets. Jenny's your coach but she's got you on the bench, playing second string. You only get to play a few downs and no one gets to see your potential. I'm inviting you to come throw the ball for the Dolphins. With the Dolphins, you're going to be the starting quarterback. You're going to play every offensive down for every game. You're going to experience all the glory, and you're going to celebrate the Super Bowl. Do you know why?"

He looked at me, smiling.

"I'm your coach. I'm going to look after you. You're my priority and I'll do whatever it takes to get you everything you want and everything you need to be more successful."

Dr. John became my pure Red doctor for Spurdisel. He wrote more than 100 prescriptions each month, contributing to my climbing up the ranks of top salespeople for Stansel Pharmaceuticals. As anticipated, other reps took notice and asked my secret for growing market share so quickly.

SELLING: HARD LESSONS LEARNED
Alec Burlakoff/ Training@aburlakoff.com

"I've got the best speaker on the planet," I told them. "You won't get better than Dr. John if you want to educate other doctors on the value of Spurdisel."

Dr. John's speaking career took off, allowing him to get what he wanted: spending more time with fewer patients, without sacrificing his income. And I got what I wanted, which was a higher level of respect from Dr. John. He in turn wrote more prescriptions for Spurdisel.

By repeating my pattern of developing Red doctors, I became the top sales rep at Stansel. It felt great to reach the top of my game as a rep for big pharma. My reputation in the industry grew. And it didn't take long for opportunities in biotech to open.

CHAPTER 6:
MOVING TO EXCELON

Working for big pharma companies like Stevens and Williams, or Magnolia, had advantages. Those companies offered real stability, with household name recognition. Medical and non-medical staff members in any doctor's office would recognize the big-name brands. I regretted losing my career with Magnolia after nine months. But when Stevens and Williams hired me to represent Spurdisel for its Stansel division, I landed back on my feet and advanced quickly, expecting to stay with Stansel for decades.

Careers don't always align with individual expectations. An advantage of 21st-century technology is a 24-hour news cycle that delivers real-time awareness about new opportunities in the marketplace, and success makes the marketplace aware of us. In that regard, analogies can be drawn between business, careers, and sports.

Pharmaceutical companies are like teams, and sales reps are like players on the teams. The teams may win or lose depending on how much effort the players put into the game. Some players will go all-out. Other players will coast along. Standings will tell us a great deal about how teams perform. When teams need help, they will recruit stronger leadership and better players.

As a sales rep at Stansel, standings made it clear that I was performing at the top of my game. When I joined the company, the leading psychiatrists in my district of Boca Raton wrote hundreds of prescriptions for Atipal and Loquelsan. Within a few weeks I made headway. By building great relationships with leading doctors in the area, sales for Spurdisel came out of the cellar. Since pharmaceutical sales were a matter of record, anyone that followed the industry could see the correlation. When I joined Magnolia, sales for drugs I represented escalated. When I joined Stansel, sales for Spurdisel in my district started to climb.

When I started in sales with a company, I went in with the mindset of becoming a market leader.

Others in the industry took notice. Did higher sales from medications result from luck, coincidence, name recognition of big-pharma, or strong critical-thinking skills by the rep?

I'm huge believer in an old cliché:

- The harder we work, the smarter we get.

When we study our market and we apply all of our critical-thinking skills, we see how best to deploy our energy. When we know how to deploy our energy best, our performance improves. The entire team benefits.

Sometimes, a single player that truly understands the game can advance the entire team. Look at Michael Jordan during his heyday. Some would say that he carried the Chicago Bulls. The entire team benefitted from his exceptional performance. Were his earnings commensurate with his contributions?

In business, as in sports, leaders should create policies that incentivize all members of the team to play at the highest level. But in large companies, policies tend to reward seniority rather than individual performance. That scenario brought an unexpected end to my career with the Stansel Pharmaceutical division at Stevens and Williams.

TEAM SALES:

Despite the advantage of name recognition and stability, working for big-pharma companies had some disadvantages. Reliance on bureaucratic structures and long-standing policies stymies innovation. Big-pharma policies capped how much sales reps could earn in bonuses and commissions. Further, when it came to career advancement, seniority could influence outcomes. Big companies placed too much value on structure, requiring reps to work together as sales teams rather than as individuals.

SELLING: HARD LESSONS LEARNED
Alec Burlakoff/ Training@aburlakoff.com

At Magnolia, I had a territory that I shared with two other sales reps. When drug sales picked up in our district, we all stood out. Stevens and Williams had the same structure in all its divisions, including Stansel Pharmaceuticals. I worked together with Paulina in my district. When I did well, she did well. To some extent, our compensation plans aligned with how we performed together as a team rather than how we performed individually.

When the district manager, Alan, hired me at Stansel to begin representing Spurdisel, he told me that I'd be working alongside Paulina. To grow as a team, I did everything possible to develop her sales IQ. We worked well together, as evidenced by the spike in sales for Spurdisel. When outsiders assessed pharmaceutical sales records, they wouldn't know whether it was Paulina or me that drove our team.

Bryce managed a sales team at Excelon, one of Stansel's competitors. Excelon was a hungrier, nimbler pharmaceutical company without as much name recognition as Stevens and Williams. Wall Street executives categorized Excelon as a biotech company rather than big pharma. As a biotech firm, Excelon didn't have the entrenched management bureaucracy of the old, established firms like Stevens and Williams. Rather than rewarding teams or seniority, leadership at Excelon encouraged its managers to be creative. Managers wanted to find star players that would sink or swim on their own merit.

As a district manager for Excelon, Bryce scouted for star players to join his team. Research led him to Paulina, my partner at Stansel. She had been at Stansel longer than me, and in our industry, longevity would suggest that she was the more experienced and senior rep. In reality, market share for Spurdisel did not start to grow until I joined Stansel. Paulina was extremely talented but had been previously brainwashed throughout her tenure in "big pharma." She had been drinking the "Kool Aid" far too many years.

As I taught Paulina, by applying 98 percent of our energy to develop relationships with the right 2 percent of doctors, we would dominate our competitors.

About two years into my tenure of working with Paulina, she confided in me that she was going to switch jobs. Bryce had been courting her. She'd met with him a few times, and she decided to make the switch. "You should meet with Bryce," she encouraged me. "Excelon is a perfect company for you. It's all about rewarding performance and there isn't any limit on what you can earn."

SELLING: HARD LESSONS LEARNED
Alec Burlakoff/ Training@aburlakoff.com

EXCELON:

By the time Paulina told me that she'd be leaving our team, there wasn't a lot of room to grow in our market. We'd already taken Spurdisel from a 10 percent market share to an 80 percent share. There wouldn't be much upside left.

When Paulina suggested that I meet with Bryce, I wasn't too enthusiastic about leaving big-pharma. I liked the perks and name recognition. But the more she spoke about Excelon's commitment to rewarding performance, the more intrigued I became.

Even if I somehow miraculously succeeded in getting 100 percent of the market share, company policies at Stevens and Williams would cap my compensation. Since I already maxed out on commissions, I wouldn't earn any more. At Excelon, Paulina explained, there wouldn't be any cap. I would earn in accordance with my performance.

I met with Bryce and we hit it off immediately. Standing about 6-4, Bryce was a natural athlete and a great motivator. He grew up in Philadelphia and had the same Northeast swagger I felt accustomed to being around.

Before offering me the sales position with Excelon, Bryce asked what I didn't like about working with big-pharma. For the most part, it was the micro-management. I didn't like all of the regulations and structure on how the company expected me to spend my time. I had a phrase: Time / access / interest. If I could find a doctor that would give me time, access, and interest, we could grow together.

Since I was out in the field, I alone should determine how I spent my time. If I wanted to spend 98 percent of my time with 2 percent of the doctors, and the strategy led to results, the company should support my efforts. I succeeded because I would gauge a doctor's level of interest and how much access I would have to him. When I found the right Red doctor, I'd happily give him all of my time.

Bryce told me that if I joined Excelon, I would have complete autonomy on how I spent my time. Rather than trying to micromanage how I succeeded, he would give me the tools, discretion, and liberty I needed to thrive. Bryce wanted entrepreneurs, people that could innovate and think on their own about how to build market share.

When Bryce told me that all sales reps would have total independence, rather than work as part of a team, I became even more intrigued. I wouldn't have to carry anyone. If I worked hard and brought in sales, I'd earn commissions. There wouldn't be any limits. Excelon wanted to grow and the company incentivized players accordingly, with no caps on what I could earn.

SELLING: HARD LESSONS LEARNED
Alec Burlakoff/ Training@aburlakoff.com

I decided to abandon big-pharma for a more exciting career in biotech.

OFF-LABEL PHARMACEUTICALS:

Part of the reason that Excelon succeeded, from my perspective, was the creativity of its CEO, Steve Briscino. Besides having a doctorate in pharmacology, Steve impressed me as being a brilliant strategist. In the previous chapter, I wrote about the enormous investment pharmaceutical companies made to bring a drug to market. With so much engineering and testing, big-pharma would invest billions before they could begin selling drugs to consumers. Sometimes, the authorities would approve drugs for a specific type of treatment. Yet once the FDA approved a drug, doctors had enormous discretion on how they could prescribe it.

Steve Briscino saw opportunity in drugs that previously had failed miserably in the market place. Rather than risking billions of dollars to develop its own drugs, Excelon would take a more innovative approach to the market. First, it researched the properties and capabilities of FDA-approved drugs. If the FDA approved a drug, but the manufacturer wasn't succeeding in selling the drug, Excelon might consider whether the drug had other purposes. If the drug met Excelon's criteria, and if it could come to financial terms with the manufacturer, Excelon acquired the rights to the drug—sparing itself the risk associated with developmental costs.

Bryce recruited me to represent three drugs that Excelon had acquired, including:

- Quixic: Approved as an opioid-based, break-through pain drug for cancer patients.
- Gravital: Approved as an adjunct drug therapy for patients suffering from EDS associated with obstructive sleep apnea.
- Brixitiv: Approved as an NSAID drug to assist patients that struggled with partial seizures.

Although the FDA approved each of those Excelon drugs, the markets for their intended usage were relatively small. If doctors learned about the benefits of each drug, however, they had discretion to prescribe the drug for other uses. Prescribing the drug for uses other than which the FDA approved would be known as "off-label usage."

I agreed to join Bryce's team at Excelon because it seemed a perfect fit for me. By working hard, I would learn everything I could about the science behind each drug, including the various ways that each drug could benefit patients. It's crucial for me to mention that although doctors have discretion to prescribe drugs for off-label usage, rules expressly forbid pharmaceutical reps to recommend drugs for anything other than what the FDA had approved.

As an aggressive, innovative biotech company, Excelon hired reps that could think creatively. A good rep needed to understand the rules, understand the medication, and understand how to build market share. During training sessions for new-hire reps at Excelon, one out of three candidates would quit and go home. Company leaders focused all of their messaging on the science behind the drug, and the different ways it would benefit patients. Conservative reps quickly understood the underlying message. Rather than selling Quixic, Gravital, and Brixitiv for their FDA-approved usage, Excelon wanted its reps to use critical-thinking skills. If they succeeded, they would increase distributions with off-label prescriptions.

BUILDING MARKET SHARE:

Where other reps saw risk, I saw opportunity. I knew that every opportunity began with building a relationship. It followed with messaging.

By developing a relationship with a doctor, I could ascertain his what's-in-it-for-me question. Knowing a doctor's WIFM put me in a position of being able to solve problems. When I solved problems, I brought value to my customers.

Excelon gave me the tools I needed to solve problems.

Once I learned the different ways that Excelon's drugs could help patients, I knew that they would bring enormous value to any doctor. Any patient that scheduled an appointment with a doctor suffered from some kind of pain or ailment. And what did all doctor's want? They wanted successful practices. How do doctors build successful practices? By helping their patients feel better.

The average sales rep at Excelon limited his presentation on drugs for specific types of doctors. They would promote Quixic to pain doctors. They would visit doctors that treated sleeping disorders to discuss the benefits of Gravital. And they would visit miscellaneous doctors to talk about Brixitiv. After all, the FDA approved those drugs for specific reasons. Quixic treated break-through pain; Gravital treated sleep apnea, and Brixitiv treated people suffering from partial seizures. If they wanted to build prescriptions for each drug, they would need to call upon many more doctors.

I saw my role differently. And at Excelon, I had the discretion on how I would spend my time. Again, I'd give 98 percent of my attention to the 2 percent of doctors that I could help most.

SELLING: HARD LESSONS LEARNED
Alec Burlakoff/ Training@aburlakoff.com

By paying close attention to the chemists and pharmacists at Excelon, and asking the right questions, I learned a lot more about the powers of each drug that Excelon carried. Although rules prohibited me from *recommending* drugs for anything other than what the FDA approved, I could become a doctor's best friend by sharing more about what I learned. Doctors would make decisions on what best to prescribe for their patients.

I called upon pain-management doctors, including neurologists, physiatrists, and anesthesiologists. Most of the patients that went to see those doctors would suffer from chronic pain. They're always suffering, with aches that they cannot explain. Rather than prescribing one drug, I'd help those doctors understand how each Excelon drug would bring enormous value to the practice.

The FDA approved Quixic for breakthrough pain, which is an obvious benefit for a pain-management doctor. But what happens to a patient that is being treated with an opioid like Quixic? The patient's breathing slows. When the breathing slows, the patient gets tired. If a patient is always tired, the patient loses out on a quality of life. How can he go to work if he's tired all the time?

Pain-management doctors that prescribed Quixic would do well to know more about Gravital and Brixitiv. My presentations helped doctors understand that active ingredients of Gravital combatted excessive daytime sleepiness. By stopping transmitters from firing too quickly, Brixitiv slowed everything down. The short story is that Gravital kept people awake, and Brixitiv would relieve anxiety and help them sleep. Such uses may not have been the intended use, but if doctors knew more about the drugs, they could contribute to their practice. They could work wonders in conjunction with Quixic, even though the FDA approved Gravital and Brixitiv for different purposes.

Doctors had the discretion to decide what they would prescribe. In my role as a sales rep for Excelon, I only wanted the doctors with whom I spent time to know their options.

My strong relationships with doctors allowed me to speak with them bluntly. They were Red doctors, they were businessmen. They knew that patients in chronic pain needed attention, and Excelon drugs could help them. Like a carpenter needed hammers and drills and levels in the toolbox, doctors needed to have the best medications to treat their patients. I could help them understand these drugs by telling a story.

"Doc, you know what it's like when you're walking down the hallway to see a troubled patient. You've consulted the chart and you know it's huge. The patient just keeps coming back and you don't know how to treat the problem. It could be psychological, it could be physical. This patient is always

SELLING: HARD LESSONS LEARNED
Alec Burlakoff/ Training@aburlakoff.com

describing aches and pain that make him anxious and nervous. My FDA approved drug is similar to Maalox, but for the brain. If used appropriately, it can make your patients feel better. And that's what you want. By learning more and understanding the drug, you can determine whether it's right for your patient."

As a result of the investment I made in learning about the medications that Excelon offered, I could bring more values to the doctors with whom I chose to spend time. That strategy of giving 98 percent of my attention to 2 percent of the doctors I saw, would result in doctors writing for all three of my drugs every day. More often than not, it would be the same patient receiving all of these three pharmacological therapies. This I tell you, is efficiency at its very finest.

And that strategy led to my quickly becoming the number one sales rep in the nation for Excelon, a position I held for nine consecutive months.

MANAGEMENT:

My meteoric rise at Excelon didn't only lead me to the top of the sales team, it also boosted the performance of Bryce, my area manager. Bryce and I had become close personal friends, and he didn't want to lose me from his team. Yet a company like Excelon valued individual performance more than seniority. When a management position opened, even though others on Bryce's team had been with the company much longer than I had, Bryce had promoted me.

Typically, in pharmaceutical companies the Vice President of Sales reports to the CEO. The National Sales Director would oversee Regional Sales Directors and report directly to the VP of Sales. The Regional Sales Director would oversee 10 District Managers and report to the National Sales Director. The District Manager would oversee 10 sales reps and report to the Regional Sales Director.

My new position at Excelon was titled Market Development Manager. In that role, I spent half of my time overseeing the "speaker's bureau," which paid doctor's honorariums to champion our drugs. I spent the other half of my time managing large institutional accounts, including health centers, prisons, nursing homes, and military treatment facilities. That role lasted for nine months, during which time I brought in several big accounts. With that growth came a new position, as a district manager, where Excelon tasked me to hire and train my own sales reps for the first time.

The four years I spent at Excelon taught me a great deal about working with people. By then, I'd been working in the pharmaceutical space for longer than seven years. My motto was to always work toward the next promotion, or to move on to the next opportunity. And the next stop for me was with Argos Pharmaceuticals.

CHAPTER 7:
POWER AND RECOGNITION

Where are you going with your career?,

With seven years of experience in the pharmaceutical space, I started to itch for more responsibility in 2008. The compensation plan at Excelon boosted my income to the mid-six figures, allowing me to provide for our family. I was 34 years old. Stephanie would soon bring our second baby girl, into our family. It was a good time, but I wanted more power and responsibility with my career.

In earlier chapters, I wrote about the importance of values and goals. As individuals and professionals, we do better when we define success. What is it we're after? Once we know what we're after, we can chart a series of individual goals. Those incremental goals should take us from where we are to where we want to go. And if we're not going to reach those goals in time, then we either have to settle with that reality or make a change.

Understanding that pattern helped me climb the ranks in a rewarding industry. A mindset of wanting more always drove me to reach higher. When I switched from education to sales, I made the change because I knew that I needed more to provide for our family. But it wasn't only money that drove me.

Internally, at my core, I competed with both my father and my brother. Despite struggling with bi-polar disorder, and not being admitted to the law profession, my brother Ian rose to the top of his game in auto sales. He managed a large dealership and did so well that the owner carved out a small equity stake for him. He brought down a huge income of more than $700,000 annually. My father did well, too.

To mirror their success, I felt a burning desire to climb higher. The role of Sales Manager didn't satisfy the ambitions I set for myself. My mindset required constant growth and challenge. Success should always go to the winner, the one that brought in the best results. In sales, there weren't any safety nets or rewards for mediocrity. In fact, I detested mediocrity, or anyone that coasted along, trading on the success of those beneath them.

Every day I'd have to push myself to the limit, then push myself a little bit farther. I thrived on the action. And I wanted to surround myself with others that drove themselves equally as hard.

When I transitioned from leading Rep to management at Excelon, my role changed. Rather than nurturing relationships with the Red doctors I cultivated, my Director expected me to build my own team. I loved the sales aspect, and always wanted to be in the game. I took pride in saying that I would never ask anyone to do anything that I wasn't doing in my role.

The doctors I carefully selected to target didn't see me as a Rep that carried around a bag of samples. They saw me as a key asset, adding value to their practice. I helped them think differently, helped them to realize their goals of building more efficient and successful careers. By shifting that power dynamic, they accepted me as a collaborative partner rather than a pushy sales rep. We grew our businesses together.

I knew what was in it for them, and they knew what was in it for me. But if we didn't have our values and goals in alignment, we could push things too far. That didn't become clear to me until much later.

When Excelon promoted me to Sales Manager, I had new responsibilities. I had to hire, teach, motivate, and oversee a team of ten Reps. They would report directly to me, and my success would depend upon their success. If I hired slackers, or people that didn't understand the game, my career would stagnate.

Since I expected my team to outperform all others, I couldn't carry any dead weight. To get the power and recognition I wanted, I hired, trained,

SELLING: HARD LESSONS LEARNED
Alec Burlakoff/ Training@aburlakoff.com

and cultivated stars. Like my brother, I was blazing a path to reach the top of my game. If I wasn't number one in my position, I expected to be fired. But if I used all of my critical thinking skills and reached number one, then I expected to be promoted. I lived by that motto of knowing that I would either be earning my way to the next promotion or expecting to be fired. If anyone wanted job security or status quo, they should not be in sales.

To build my team of Reps, I worked harder than ever. For several weeks, I basically lived in hotel rooms, recruiting and training and motivating my team. We dominated the market, building the highest-grossing sales in the country. As a result of the successful team we built, my Regional Director outperformed his peers. When opportunities opened within the company for a new Regional Director, he had the audacity to say that he wouldn't promote me because he didn't want to lose out on the commissions my team generated.

This was the mark of B-player, and I had a choice to make. Either I could stagnate, allowing a B-player to dictate my future, or I could move on to the next opportunity.

CHANGING LANES:

The skills I developed during those first seven years in professional sales would translate to any industry. I knew it.

People in professional sales had to invest time to build super-strong critical thinking skills, showing enormous value. For a sales professional to show value, he had better learn how to sell himself first. That's the differentiator between an A-player and a B-player. An A-player knows that he is the product. If he doesn't grasp how to help the customer know, like, and trust him, then he had better find a different career. When an A-player is the product, then the company had better make sure opportunities are always opening for him to succeed. Otherwise, the company will lose A-players and spiral into mediocrity.

When it became clear that my Regional Director wanted to continue reaping the rewards of the successful team I built, and that he would block my pathway to becoming a Director, I lost interest. I earned good money in the role, but success meant more than money. I needed to build, to grow, to reach the highest potential possible. I couldn't live with myself if I allowed B-players to hinder growth for the company I represented or for my career.

SELLING: HARD LESSONS LEARNED
Alec Burlakoff/ Training@aburlakoff.com

ARGOS DIAGNOSTICS:

One of my colleagues, Mark, introduced me to the leadership team at Argos Diagnostics. Mark and I used to work together at Ridge Pines. When I transitioned into pharmaceuticals and saw the earning opportunities, I suggested that Mark join me. Within six months, Mark sold pharmaceuticals alongside me. Over the next several years, he rose in the ranks, eventually becoming a Sales Manager with his own team of Reps at Argos Diagnostics.

Argos, a division of a large, publicly traded healthcare conglomerate, aspired to grow. In search of a new leader, they reached out to Mark. They knew that Mark understood the "whatever-it-took" philosophy. But by 2008, Mark had left Argos to become president of American Scientific. In his new role, Mark settled into a comfortable position that didn't require any travel or pressure. When Argos recruited Mark to return as the National Sales Director, he passed. Instead, he recommended me. "You should hire Alec," Mark told them. "No one is more qualified to boost sales at Argos. I trained under him and I'm confident that you'll be impressed with his passion and energy."

With Mark's recommendation, Argos started to recruit me aggressively. National Sales Director would be a big step, requiring our family to move to Boston. In my mind, one of the best jobs in pharmaceutical sales would be Regional Director, which was the role I wanted at Excelon.

A Regional Director oversaw 10 Sales Managers, each of whom oversees 10 Reps. He worked from home and basically kept a big team in line, without having to get bogged down with too much interference from corporate headquarters. From my perspective, Regional Director would have been an ideal position because I could spend time with my family while simultaneously cultivating a team of 100 A-players.

Argos offered me the higher position of National Sales Director, requiring more responsibility. I'd oversee 10 Regional Directors, that oversaw 10 Sales Managers, that oversaw 10 Reps. The role would require that I work closely with the VP of Sales, based out of the corporate headquarters. I saw possible advantages and disadvantages. The main advantage would be that I could drive my own ship, but the disadvantage would be that our family would need to relocate to Boston so I could work in the corporate headquarters. I didn't like the idea of being stuck behind a desk.

In 2008, Argos generated about $30 million in quarterly revenues from diagnostics testing. The company wanted to grow revenues, but it didn't have a plan. I had all the qualifications to deliver results, and quickly. They put me through a battery of psychological tests and a series of interviews. At

SELLING: HARD LESSONS LEARNED
Alec Burlakoff/ Training@aburlakoff.com

every stage, I laid out a precise philosophy of how I would grow sales.

During each face-to-face interview, I let the team know my philosophy for building a killer end-user sales force. The secret would always be to find the WIFM. To understand the WIFM, a professional Rep would need to know how to build relationships. Without strong relationships, a Rep could never change the power dynamic. Reps need skill sets that lead to becoming a trusted colleague of the doctor. If the doctor didn't have that trust, I explained, there would never be anything more than a "transactional" relationship.

NO WOLF OF WALL STREET

In 2013, Leonardo DiCaprio starred in *The Wolf of Wall Street*. The movie glamorized crazy excess in a boiler-room sales environment. Rather than building trusting relationships, the people in that movie manipulated and deceived. Every time they made a call, they were after a sales transaction, and the client knew it. The element of trust didn't exist. Every call was about a sale, a one-call close, a transaction predicated on the greed for more money, or the fear of losing money.

To build higher sales at Argos Diagnostics, I explained, we needed a sales force that understood how to connect with highly educated, conservative professionals. Doctors would not respond to hype. They would do business with people they trusted, not with people that only wanted to sell or conduct immediate transactions.

As a National Sales Director, I would expect everyone on my team to do whatever it took to build solid relationships with physicians. They had to embrace the 98/2 rule, concentrating their time on building relationships with the *right* physicians. In other words, they needed to build their own stable of Red doctors, and they would need me to provide them with both the resources and the independence to succeed.

I wanted to cultivate a sales team that understood the value of rejection. Hearing the word "no" would be one of the best things that could happen to a salesperson. Why? Because a professional salesperson knew and understood that if he were going to be successful, he had to spend 98 percent of his time with 2 percent of available clients. The sooner a doctor told or showed him that he wasn't worth the effort, the sooner a salesperson could move on to the next prospective candidate.

Time would be value, but discretion would also be valuable. To succeed as an A-player in sales, a person needed to hone critical-thinking skills—always in search of that 2 percent. He had to take every call from his Red doctors, and he had to meet on his or her terms.

SELLING: HARD LESSONS LEARNED
Alec Burlakoff/ Training@aburlakoff.com

The team at Argos liked what they heard. They hired me as National Sales Director in the fall of 2008, when I was 34. While Stephanie advanced through a difficult pregnancy that kept her bedridden for several months, I commuted to Boston to get started on the job.

DIAGNOSTICS VERSUS PHARMACEUTICALS

As I saw it, healthcare sales had three separate subsectors. Medical devices, including orthopedics, stints, or other types of equipment doctors used to treat patients. Another vertical in the space included pharmaceuticals and medications, where I had developed expertise. The third subsector would be diagnostics. Medical diagnostics is the process of determining which diseases or conditions explain a person's symptoms.

Argos Diagnostics offered more than 400 types of blood tests for rare genetic disorders.

When I moved to Boston to begin training for my new role, I studied the exhaustive category of available tests. Patients or insurance companies would pay fees of $1,000 to $20,000 per genetic test. Extensive amounts of literature, replete with fine print, would describe the tests.

I realized the magnitude of my job. The sales team I intended to build would not open relationships with literature that required magnifying glasses to read. To become best in class, we needed to create a story behind each test, a story that would help a doctor recognize how prescribing the diagnostic blood test would benefit his practice. If we could create those stories, our team would become more successful at growing sales for Argos.

First, the reps would earn trust. With trust, they could find the doctor's WIFM. Then, they would show how using Argos Diagnostics would help doctors build more successful practices. If each Regional Director could master the process and teach Sales Managers that would in turn teach Reps, we would grow revenues faster than ever before.

Reps also needed to develop a skillset for weaving stories together. With stories, we help doctors relate to the patient in need. We help them visualize how our diagnostic tests lead to more effective prescriptions that improve the patient's health.

When I laid this plan out for the leadership at Argos, they expressed enthusiasm for the vision. But they didn't have any idea for what I was about to bring.

During those first weeks at Argos, I had to learn more science than ever before, and I had to learn faster. Genetic testing is extremely complicated. Since I wanted to get started quickly, I used the same 98/2 approach that I used in sales. In other words, I spent 98 percent of my time studying 2 percent of the tests that Argos offered. I had to choose the right 2 percent. Argos had tests on many categories, including epilepsy, hearing, obesity, dementia, and so forth. Too many genetic tests to learn, unless I wanted to become a scientist.

Rather than studying random tests, I focused on strengths. Always start with the low-hanging fruit! By learning what I needed to know about the tests that would best suit the doctors with whom I had existing relationships, I could bring immediate value.

As has happened with every other position I took, those first three months became a whirlwind of sales activity. Since I commuted between our home in Florida and Argos' headquarters in Boston, I made the best use of my time in either place. While in Boston I spent time with chemists to make sure I understood the five or six diagnostic tests I wanted to master. While in Florida, I worked closely with Bill, a Rep that had been with Argos for years. He was a fish out of water.

Argos belonged to that group of pharmaceutical companies that didn't want their sales reps to practice the relationship model of selling. Instead, they wanted reps to use their literature and sell the science. Bill didn't know how to sell without focusing on the science. He didn't realize that regardless of what a person sold, professional sales required building relationships. Without building solid relationships, no one could create mutually beneficial synergies.

Immediately, I disrupted his process. If Bill wanted to crush through sales goals, he needed to get out into the marketplace and build relationships. Doctors were busy and they wouldn't take time to read literature. They'd make time to spend with friends, but they wouldn't waste time on the fine print unless they had a reason. Relationships were the key to providing that reason.

While in Florida, I scheduled lunches, dinners, and quality weekend outings with doctors, bringing Bill along with me for on-the-job training. Rather than embracing the new sales strategy, he complained that he didn't like working nights and weekends. Wrong attitude!

Becoming a great sales professional requires a person to push himself beyond the comfort zone. I taught on the importance of becoming comfortable with uncomfortable conversations. If a person wasn't willing to go beyond, to ask uncomfortable questions, then the person could never become an A-player in the sales game.

There isn't any shame in being rejected or pushed out. I taught Bill the importance of being open and transparent, of letting the doctor know that he was out to earn business. We have to be methodical, intelligent. We should be clean shaven, well dressed, presentable with doctors. If doctors saw us as being on their level, we made it easier for them to relate with us.

Likewise, when we spent time with a doctor's staff members, we shouldn't be overdressed. Wherever we are, we need our audience to relate to us, on their level. That's why we work evenings with dinners, or weekends. We show doctors that we're intuitive, that we're thinking about them and their needs. We strive to help them become more successful, and in turn, we become more successful.

As Bill started to come around, his sales accelerated. In fact, they exploded. He'd been at the bottom of Argos' sales rankings for years. But within three months of the time that I landed the job, Argos' sales for diagnostic testing went from $30 million to more than $60 million. It was no by coincidence that Bill went from being a bottom feeder fighting for his job, to the number one producing rep in the country. My red targets proved their worth once again. They seemed to be the gift that kept on giving. Ahh loyalty, it's a beautiful thing.

Ironically, the sales growth alarmed the leadership at Argos. Regardless of what I had told them in the past, they didn't grasp the power of relationship selling. During every interview, I explained how my strategy of building relationships, understanding WIFMs, and overdelivering on expectations would boost sales. That is what the leadership team said they wanted. I told them that I intended to bring results, and to bring them fast. And within three months, putting a heavy focus on only 6 diagnostic tests out of more than 400 that Argos offered, my team succeeded in doubling sales. It was as if a sales hurricane had started blowing through the company, and it wasn't going to stop.

From my perspective, we were doing everything right. In fact, we were on fire, moving in the right direction. Our success, however, threatened the reputation of the VP of Sales, my direct supervisor. Rather than encouraging the growth, he tried to slow me down, depriving me of resources like funds for honorariums. It didn't make any sense. Then I realized that he was a B-player. Seeing others succeed threatened the performance (or under performance) record he built when he served as National Sales Director.

STARTING OVER

I returned to Florida on a Thursday to spend time with my family. I was three months into my career with Argos, just before we were about to make the move to Boston. Stephanie told me that tests had revealed the gender of our baby and we were going to have another daughter.

SELLING: HARD LESSONS LEARNED
Alec Burlakoff/ Training@aburlakoff.com

Since the start of the series, we enjoyed watching every episode of The Sopranos together. Everything about that show intrigued me. Tony Soprano may have been a master criminal, but he was a complex character. Despite his flaws, he would do anything for his family. His daughter, Meadow was beautiful and smart. In her real life, the actress playing Meadow was Jewish. I told Stephanie that if we ever had another daughter, I wanted to name her after Meadow Soprano.

While we looked forward to this next chapter in our life, I got summoned for a conference call with the leadership team in Boston. Despite my performance of growing sales quickly, they told me that they didn't think we were a good fit. By the end of the call, Argos had severed its relationship with me.

It was the second time I lost a job in the pharmaceutical industry. I would start a new story.

CHAPTER 8:
AMERICAN SCIENTIFIC

Things didn't work out at Argos, but that's life. Every day, we're confronted with conflicts that force us to go in different directions. If we're prepared, then it's no problem. If we're not prepared, then we face challenges.

I faced challenges.

When I lost my position with Magnolia, back in 2001, Stephanie and I were celebrating the birth of our first daughter. Argos parted ways with me at a similarly important time of our lives. Stephanie and I were bringing our second baby daughter, into the world when I learned I'd be out of a job.

Losing a steady paycheck hurt. When we have responsibilities to care for our family, the challenge is infinitely harder. My father always taught that the longer a person stayed out of the workforce, the more difficult it would be to find a job. As a result of what I learned from him, I always wanted to be employed. When we're not moving forward, we're sliding backwards.

Although I over delivered on what Argos expected from me, I saw signs early on that we were not a good fit. Despite the leadership team telling

SELLING: HARD LESSONS LEARNED
Alec Burlakoff/ Training@aburlakoff.com

me that they wanted to grow sales, escalating revenues too quickly frightened others in the company. They didn't think anyone could bring new revenues in so quickly without making ethical compromises.

But what is the essence of ethics? Isn't it doing the right thing? Isn't it being proud of delivering value that the customer wanted in an honest way?

I grew sales for Argos by understanding my customer. Their patients would benefit from a better understanding of genetic testing, and the doctors' practices would benefit by understanding more about our diagnostic tests. Argos' practice of giving literature to a busy doctor equated to adding another book in the library. Words on a page don't matter unless someone chooses to read them.

Doctors were busy. They didn't have time to read pamphlets or sit with sales reps of any kind. But they would set time aside to visit with a friend. If we built great relationships with doctors, opportunities would open for us to tell them about our services. No lying, no cheating, no manipulating. In any complex sales process, building great relationships results in better outcomes.

During the interview process, I told the team at Argos that I intended to use all of my talents and skills to build sales. They hired me to serve as a National Sales Director. What they really wanted, I think, was an operations director. If I were to sit in my chair at the corporate office studying charts and discussing strategy, they may have been happier. But "talking" about what we could do wasn't in my nature. When I accepted the job as a sales leader, I intended to take immediate steps to build a killer sales team.

Despite growing sales faster than anyone expected, the leadership team gave me signals along the way. They were slow in delivering resources I needed, stalling progress. No big deal. It wasn't a good fit.

Although I lost the steady paycheck at the same time we were growing our family with a new child, I had to adjust. Everyone needs to adjust when circumstances change.

The question is how do we do it? Do we adjust in a principled, methodical way that is consistent with our value structure and how we define success? Sometimes, when we're weak, we compromise and take the easy way out.

In retrospect, after having gone through ups and down of building a career that generated more than $3 billion in sales, I know I've learned many lessons. For me, the customer always came first. With my 100% commitment of wanting to serve the customer, I sometimes made the bad decision of compromising principles that should have guided all my decisions. Strength comes from making principled decisions.

In my case, it didn't matter what the customer wanted. I would always find a way to say yes. Staying loyal to my customer became my true north star, my compass. Others, like my friend Peter, operated by a different set of principles, as I'll describe below.

At various stages through our career, we should stop and take a personal inventory. We should make a decision on whether the choices we're making align with our values and goals, with the way that we're defining success in our life. When we make decisions that don't align with our principles, we're compromising. We're exposing ourselves to vulnerabilities. By not taking that inventory, or assessing how and why I made decisions, I created some catastrophic problems.

As I look back, problems that eventually resulted in my losing millions of dollars, my liberty, and my good name, really began after I left Argos Diagnostics. I felt so pressured to get a job right away that I took the first position that opened, with American Scientific. That position transitioned into a series of events that spiraled out of control.

AMERICAN SCIENTIFIC:

American Scientific led the market in diagnostic testing for dialysis patients. My friend Peter ran the company. When Argos began its search for a National Sales Director, Peter was their number-one candidate. Despite the great opportunity, Peter declined the offer. Instead, he recommended that Argos hire me. Peter knew and understood that he had expertise and strength in operations. He made principled decisions to protect the business he led.

Peter and I had worked together and been friends ever since we worked at The Ridge Pines School, much earlier in our careers. When I made a switch to pharmaceutical sales, he joined me at Magnolia. Later, we went our separate ways but we always remained friends. I appreciated Peter for thinking of me with the opportunity at Argos opened, and I kept him in the loop as I made the transition.

When Argos didn't work out for me, Peter suggested that I join a startup division that two of his colleagues at American Scientific wanted to launch. The switch was the first in a series of compromises I began making after leaving Argos. I took the job for the primary reason that I did not want to be unemployed. Perhaps I should have thought more about the direction I wanted my career to go.

In retrospect, I would advise anyone to make more methodical, deliberate decisions. A career choice comes with enormous opportunity costs. If we move in one direction, we move farther away from possibilities that could open in another direction.

MOBILE DIAGNOSTICS FOR SLEEP STUDIES:

Dr. Tom Roth owned American Scientific, and he trusted Peter to run the company. Besides being a physician, Tom enjoyed seizing business opportunities. Along with his close friend, Dr. Ike Cohen, Tom saw an opening to expand markets for American Scientifics by forming a new company that would offer an innovative approach to sleep diagnostics. As a neurologist, Dr. Cohen, specialized in sleep studies, and he would serve as the medical director of the new company. They wanted Peter to run operations. Provided that Tom hire me to lead sales, Peter agreed to take on the new responsibility. Without sales, Peter knew that businesses couldn't operate, and he wasn't going to divert his attention from the dialysis business.

Until American Scientific expanded with its new sleep division, patients had to go to a laboratory to get tested. The challenge, of course, was that people wanted to sleep in their own beds, in their own homes—not in a laboratory. If a physician prescribed a sleep study for a patient, the patient was reluctant to go. If the patient refused to go the laboratory for the sleep study, the doctor would never get the data necessary to diagnose the patient's various sleep disorders.

Our startup solved that problem by creating a mobile sleep lab. We purchased portable devices that our technicians would wheel into the patient's home. A technician would visit the patient in his or her home, attach the appropriate leads to the patient, and our technology would record data remotely. As medical director, Dr. Cohen would interpret and authenticate the study, making our tests much more convenient for the patient.

I used the same techniques that I had used throughout my career to catapult sales of sleep studies for American Scientific. As you might guess, I began with a clear understanding of WIFM. In order to get doctors to prescribe our mobile sleep studies, I had to consider how our product would benefit their practices.

SYNERGIES:

When making transitions, we should rely upon our strengths to accelerate progress. As sales professionals, our biggest strength is the relationships we build with our customers. When we invest time and energy to build relationships, and we do it effectively, we create a renewable asset. As long as we understand how our customers prosper, we can use our intelligence to help them create more value.

My background in pharmaceutical sales gave me enormous insight into pain points that my Red doctors faced. They wanted to treat patients quickly and efficiently. But if they didn't have the tools they needed, they faced obstacles. In my new role as the sales leader for American Scientific, I could remove obstacles for old customers with whom I'd developed outstanding relationships. If I called upon them, they would listen.

As I described in a previous chapter, Excelon specialized in acquiring rights to sell FDA-approved pharmaceuticals that had been performing poorly in the marketplace. The nimble biotech company intended to capitalize on their acquisitions by boosting sales of drugs for "off-label" purposes. When I was a sales rep at Excelon, I had to be creative. Although a doctor could prescribe any approved medication, sales reps were forbidden from suggesting off-label usage for any medication.

The FDA had approved Excelon's brand drug, Vigil, as an adjunct therapy for obstructive sleep apnea. Regardless of whether there was a diagnosis for sleep apnea, doctors could prescribe the drug for any purpose they deemed appropriate. But insurance companies wouldn't pay for any name-brand medication unless the doctor prescribed it for the narrow purpose that the FDA approved. That pain point complicated life for a true Red doctor. I remember doctors telling me:

"Alec I'd love to prescribe Vigil to my patients. It's perfect for them, especially since it's not a schedule 2 drug. My patients love Vigil because it helps them combat excessive daytime sleepiness as a result of their around-the-clock opioid therapy. But insurance companies won't approve payment for the drug without a diagnosis for sleep apnea. So I could write prescriptions all day, but if insurance companies won't pay for Vigil, it won't matter. Patients won't pay for a brand-drug like Vigil if they have to pay for it out of pocket."

To accelerate sales for our new mobile diagnostics service, I began calling upon the Key Opinion Leaders I had cultivated in pain management over the course of my career. Those doctors knew me. They loved me. The doctors understood that if I were calling them, I must have a solution to improve efficiencies in their practice. They knew I respected their time and wouldn't waste their energy if I didn't know I could bring value.

I showed how our innovative mobile sleep-study equipment would get their patients the diagnosis they needed for sleep apnea. Once they were diagnosed with sleep apnea, doctors could prescribe Vigil and the insurance companies would have to pay for the prescription.

SELLING: HARD LESSONS LEARNED
Alec Burlakoff/ Training@aburlakoff.com

The synergy between doctor, patient, and the new company resulted in an explosion of sales for American Scientific. Such growth would not have transpired without the key relationships I'd invested time to build and nurture.

What's the takeaway here?

As sales professionals, we need to know every aspect of our market and we also must know the business model of our customers. In this case, look at the value created as a direct result of the investment I made by building relationships with physicians. I understood that physicians wanted to serve patients, but I also understood the challenges they were facing from insurance companies. Although I didn't have to work directly with insurance companies, I served my customers better by learning how to solve challenges they faced. Relationships I built over years gave me the privilege of being able to speak with them about innovative ideas. Mobile sleep studies was a concept that hadn't previously existed before American Scientific introduced them into the marketplace. On account of the credibility I had earned, doctors were willing to listen when I pitched them on the value our services could provide.

Doctors with whom I had built relationships prescribed at-home sleep tests for all of their patients. As Key Opinion Leaders, those doctors influenced their colleagues to do the same. As a result of all those prescriptions, within six months of launching, we became the dominant sleep-diagnostics service in our region, disrupting the entire industry.

DISRUPTION:

Sales can be a zero-sum game. If one rep gets a sale, that means another rep lost a potential customer. Frank owned nine separate sleep laboratories. As a result of our success, Frank's business started a steady decline in revenues. He could have tried to compete by developing a mobile testing service of his own, but without a deep roster of Red doctors to call upon, he would face hurdles getting traction.

After nine months of being creamed in the market, Frank tried a different approach. He called Peter to warn him about potential danger in the marketplace. Being an operations guy, Peter didn't want anything to threaten American Scientific's dominance in providing diagnostics for dialysis patients. We had success with the launch of our sleep-study venture, but Peter was very clear in what was most important to him. To learn more about Frank's admonitions, Peter and I agreed to join him for a dinner meeting.

Both of us understood that Frank had his own agenda. Our rapid success threatened the viability of Frank's business. Patients would not go for overnight testing in a laboratory if they could be tested

SELLING: HARD LESSONS LEARNED
Alec Burlakoff/ Training@aburlakoff.com

at home. Not wanting to lose any more business to the innovative service we introduced into the marketplace, Frank asked for the meeting. Clearly, he hoped that through a discussion, he could find some sort of solution that would save his business.

Frank was friendly, but he questioned the legality of what we were doing. He said that neither Medicare nor other insurance providers had authorized the type of mobile sleep studies we were conducting. Insurance companies paid for patients that stayed in overnight labs that regulatory agencies like the Joint Commission had approved. Since American Scientific did not have clarification from insurance companies, Peter was appropriately concerned.

Following that dinner, Peter and I discussed the risks.

Insurance providers didn't say that we could not bill for our sleep studies, but neither did they say our sleep studies were authorized. There was a risk that regulators could shut us down, or refuse to pay for the services we provided. If that happened, the disruption could threaten Peter's extremely successful dialysis business.

Frank's company would not have such problems. Since regulatory agencies had already approved of the service that Frank offered, his established company would not have any problems with billing. To avoid regulatory problems, Frank suggested that American Scientific get out of the sleep-study business entirely. If Peter would sell, Frank offered to pay a fair price for all of American Scientific's equipment and hire me to run his mobile division.

MAKING VALUES-BASED DECISIONS:

Despite the rapidly growing sales that I was bringing in, Peter made principled decisions. He had clear insight on what was important to him and he wouldn't deviate from his course. I admired that about Peter. When Argos offered him a big position of leading a national sales team, he knew that a sales position would not align with the principles by which he was living. He no longer wanted to interact directly with customers.

Within days of joining American Scientific, I brought sales at a level that vastly exceeded expectations. Nevertheless, within days of Frank making a case suggesting that regulators could have a problem with our mobile-testing devices, Peter decided to shut the business down. His boss, Dr. Roth wanted Peter to push the envelope a bit and try to keep the sleep business going. Peter defied him, refusing to budge on his principles. If Dr. Roth wanted Peter to run American Diagnostics, Peter would only do it his way—without any hint of controversy or do-

SELLING: HARD LESSONS LEARNED
Alec Burlakoff/ Training@aburlakoff.com

ing anything that others might construe as violating ethical principles.

I wasn't nearly as principled, and I regret it.

With Peter's blessing, I left American Diagnostics to join Frank's company. When I joined, I introduced him to my concept of "the money hours." Mediocre reps believe that work hours begin at nine and end at five. In reality, if a person wants to reach the top of his game, he's got to be ready to work anytime, especially before nine and after five. Those are the money hours. We don't want to be calling upon our customers at the time when they're interacting with patients. Our job is to make things easier for them, to see them when we're not interfering with their practice.

There was never a time when I didn't have my cell phone with me, especially when I was introducing a new product like the mobile sleep study. I'd push myself hard, striving to build new relationships. Some sales trainers mistakenly talk about sales as being a marathon, as we've should pace ourselves. I advised just the opposite. When we're blasting into a new market, we've got to ramp sales up quickly. We've got to go through a series of sprints. We should push ourselves as hard as we're able, to the point where we're almost getting sick. If we need to slow down, we give ourselves a day of rest so we can recalibrate. As soon as our energy comes back, we get right back out there and do it again.

As a result of the heavy push I made, Frank and I grew his company into a formidable force. By running nine sleep laboratories, he had limitations. He could only accept as many patients as his laboratories would hold. But with our new mobile division, we eliminated those limitations. We could take on as many patients as doctors would prescribe.

CHANGES IN THE MARKETPLACE:

After a few years of doing well with Frank's company, insurance companies changed their payment policies for mobile sleep studies. We had a great run for a while. Yet the changing economics threatened my earning potential. Since insurance companies were going to pay less for mobile-diagnostic services, my compensation would drop. Frank suggested that while I should stay on with his company, I ought to look for opportunities that might supplement my income.

These are the dynamics that led to the next phase of my career, with Ingrid Therapeutics.

CHAPTER 9:
INGRID

Ingrid Biologics, a biotech company based in Arizona, had not been on my radar as a potential employer. In fact, if things would've gone my way, I would've continued developing my career with Frank. By growing the mobile-diagnostics division, we created unbelievable efficiencies that served both the patients and the doctors well. But when insurance companies cut the rates that they would pay, everything changed in the market.

Frank and I wanted to continue working together. Yet whenever markets change, we all need to be ready to adjust to the changing landscape and circumstances.

Too many people follow the pathway of the ostrich. When on ostrich senses danger, it quickly digs a hole and buries its head in the sand. Lions may approach. By hiding its head in the sand, the ostrich can't see anything. Since the ostrich can't see anything, it deludes itself into believing that the lion won't see anything either. That strategy doesn't work out so well for the ostrich. A strategy of burying our head in the sand won't work out so well for anyone else, either. We've got to face challenges head on.

SELLING: HARD LESSONS LEARNED
Alec Burlakoff/ Training@aburlakoff.com

Until Frank and I could create new opportunities to work together, he encouraged me to supplement my income with independent consulting projects. Frank pledged to accommodate my schedule, providing the time off I would need. We both understood that changing economics in the sleep-diagnostics industry meant that in time, he would have to cut my pay until we created new ventures and new profits.

In that climate, I heard about Ingrid Biologics from Tara. Tara and I had worked together previously and we always stayed in touch. She contributed as a top producer on the sales team I developed at Excelon several years earlier. While at Excelon, I groomed Tara to be a sales rep and she performed really well. Intuitively, Tara understood the concept of the 98/2 rule, developing relationships with physicians perfectly. I admired her work ethic.

Any sales professional that adheres to the 98/2 rule had better have a great relationship with the sales manager. Some sales managers insist that their sales reps "work hard" by adhering to a regimen of calling on all customers equally.

Anyone that wants to succeed has to work hard. That's a given. But hard work doesn't absolve us from our responsibility to think. We've got to be smart. We've got to know that by using strong critical-thinking skills, we identify where to spend our time and how to spend our time. Success isn't about working nine-to-five, or about calling everyone in the phone book. It's about using our intelligence, understanding the opportunity costs that accompany every decision.

While at Excelon, Tara understood that if she called upon 100 doctors, only 2 would meet her specific criteria as being candidates that could deliver results. If she found the right two doctors, on the other hand, they would deliver better results than the other 98 combined. To operate in such a manner, she needed the right manager, she needed a manager that would give her discretion to sink or swim based upon the sales that came in from decisions she made.

When Tara joined Ingrid, she saw an opportunity and urged me to come on board. If I were her manager, she said, there wouldn't be any limit to how much she could earn.

Ingrid, she told me, was run by Jim Shastry, an ambitious billionaire who successfully built a few other biotech companies. He launched Ingrid with his own capital. The FDA had recently given Ingrid a patent for an innovative, spray-type, drug-delivery system. At Ingrid, Shastry intended to use his patent to make more pharmaceutical drugs available through spray delivery. It's like a Binaca spray, making the medication faster-acting.

SELLING: HARD LESSONS LEARNED
Alec Burlakoff/ Training@aburlakoff.com

Ingrid used the new spray-delivery system with its drug called Stetsine, which competed with a similar drug that we sold at Excelon.

The FDA approved Stetsine for the narrow use of treating breakthrough pain for cancer patients. Tara understood that with the newly patented, spray-delivery system, Stetsine, Ingrid Biologics would have a competitive advantage in the marketplace. A quick spray under the tongue allowed the patient to absorb medicine much more efficiently. Patients would get immediate results because of the way the body could absorb the medication. By contrast, Excelon's equivalent drug was only available in lozengier form, similar to a lollipop. A lozengier would have to dissolve, and a patient would not feel relief for perhaps 15 minutes.

Tara told me that Ingrid had recently fired its VP of sales, and the leadership team was looking for candidates to build a sales force. She knew that I would be a strong candidate and urged me to meet with the principals at Ingrid. Confident that I could build the company's salesforce easily and put policies in place to accelerate growth, I agreed to fly out to Arizona to meet with Paul Wilson, the CEO for a face to face.

SELLING: HARD LESSONS LEARNED
Alec Burlakoff/ Training@aburlakoff.com

RESTAURANT INTERVIEW:

We agreed to meet at Rizzuto's, a high-end, Italian restaurant that the founder of Ingrid Biologics owned as a side business. As an experienced sales professional, I knew that an interview in a restaurant had implications. Paul Wilson would be assessing everything about me, from the second I walked in. Rather than testing my knowledge of chemistry or pharmaceuticals, I anticipated that he'd be assessing my personality and charm. Offsite interviews were informal, more about how a candidate carried himself than about what the candidate knew about a particular position.

As anticipated, Paul sat at the bar beside his close friend Tom. Tom worked as a VP of sales for a large technology company. They both welcomed me warmly, though I sensed that Paul asked his friend Tom to join us so that he could offer an independent assessment. Did I have the temperament, or presence to build a wildly successful salesforce?

While they slammed $300 shots of Sazerac, I took off my tie and glasses so they could see me as one of them—a guy that would know how to start conversations and move effortlessly between topics that didn't have anything to do with job specifics.

When I started my career with Magnolia Pharmaceuticals, the same hiring manager interviewed me three times. He said that although I gave him textbook responses to his questions during the interviews, he never got a sense of who I was as an individual. I never made that mistake again. My designer suit, matching Ferragamo shoes and belt, all said something about how I would carry myself. To trust me with representing the company, they would need to know more about my mind, personality, and sense of discretion. Together, they'd try to take a look "inside," assessing whether I was the right man, whether I had the drive, passion, and energy to lead.

Despite the casual atmosphere, I had to keep my guard. In that respect, I was like a boxer, always throwing jobs with my guard up and ready to block. I understood that they'd measure every word. As my interviewers, they could talk about taboo subjects, including women, drugs, or even laugh at their inappropriate jokes. I had to read the situation, instantly determining when to laugh, when to smirk, when to nod silently or follow up with a story of my own. They could curse, I could not. They could cross a line divulging information that would be inappropriate for me to reveal at that stage.

I had to look for opportunities where I could squeeze in responses that would slam home the message that I'm the perfect guy to get the job done. At that stage, I didn't even know for certain whether I wanted the job. But if it was a good fit, if it would provide a bridge of supplemental income I could use until Frank and I found the next venture we could work on together, I wanted to make sure that I'd have the option.

What's most important to you?

What's your approach to closing a sale?

How hard of a worker are you?

Any experienced sales professional could hit it out of the park with those type of softball questions. Interviewers expect candidates for leadership positions to know how to respond. When they ask to meet for dinner and drinks, they're assessing whether the candidate is going to fall into a trap. Like if he's going to badmouth someone else, feed into conversations that could get a company into trouble, or perhaps drink too much.

After three hours together, I felt good. They drove me to my hotel and when I got out of the car, Paul told me that he looked forward to seeing me the next day for the formal interview. He said it would be a seamless process if I chose to join the sales team. I went to bed confident, thinking that the job would be mine if I wanted it and knowing that I could succeed at the position easily.

I decided to play it out, to see how the more formal interview would go, which would be with Paul and Jim Shastry, the founder of Ingrid Biologics.

SELLING: HARD LESSONS LEARNED
Alec Burlakoff/ Training@aburlakoff.com

FORMAL INTERVIEW:

As we sat in the conference room, Jim looked over my resume and asked about earlier positions I held with Magnolia, Stevens & Williams, and Excelon. At each job, I rose to the top. I brought my "brag deck," showing numerous awards celebrating me as the top pharmaceutical sales representative or manager. Regardless of what role I had, at which company, I drove forward with a high intensity and a 100% commitment to be the lead guy.

Shastry seemed most interested on the strategy and tactics I used to develop speakers. He wanted to know how I had built a stable of doctors that actively promoted drugs I represented for different companies. Building relationships with the right doctors, I explained, made all the difference. Those doctors bought into me as an individual more than they bought into the companies that employed me.

They didn't see me as a pharmaceutical sales rep, I explained, they saw me as an asset to their practice. I brought them the tools they needed to build more profitable businesses. If a sales rep asked them to become a speaker, the doctor wouldn't listen. That's why it was so important to build relationships, friendships. I understood the WIFM, I told Shastry, and I understood which doctor would work best alongside me. I always had a stable of four or five premier speakers, and another half dozen that I was always grooming for the next opportunity. From the doctor's perspective, I didn't represent the pharmaceutical company. I knew what was important to them, and I would do anything possible to deliver. For that reason, the doctors saw me more as a partner than as a vendor.

Shastry slammed his hand down on the table, telling Wilson, "We've just met the man that's going to become our new VP of sales."

But they weren't interviewing me for the role of VP of sales. They wanted me to start off as a Sales Manager, overseeing a team of 10 sales reps. If I did well in that role, opportunities would open. The starting pay, they said, would be $80,000 per year plus a 10-percent commission. They knew that the base pay amounted to less than half the salary I was worth, and they wondered whether it would present a problem for me.

If I were in their shoes, I'd wonder too.

From my perspective, a base salary didn't matter at all. In fact, I considered it insulting to think about base salaries, or average compensation. Too many candidates go into a new-hire situation with the wrong questions in mind. They want to know about potential vacation time, about what the average guy on the job earned, about potential benefits. Those types of inquiries revealed a real problem. When candidates looked for answers about what they've got coming, they're telling the leader one thing:

- "I'm not an A-player."

An A-player knows that a winner is only worth what he brings to the table. Questions about what I thought about base pay, or what the average guy earned revealed a lack of confidence. I told them that I lived by the motto of promote me or fire me. Making it in sales meant that a guy had to have a sixth sense, knowing that he would find the way to be number-one on the team. With that in mind, the only question about earnings should be, "What does your top sales professional earn?" If I were interviewing a candidate, that was the only question I wanted to hear. After providing the answer, I'd ask his plan to reach the top.

Shastry and Wilson would want to know the same thing from me. I let them know the base pay didn't mean anything to me. They were looking for someone to build a sales team. I'm that guy. They could hire me as sales manager, but it wouldn't be long for them to see that I was cut from a different cloth. Within one month, I'd be their top guy, I told them. And then they'd be in a position of having to promote me or fire me. And once they saw the results I expected to bring, they'd realize how important it would be to make me VP of sales. When

I interviewed for the job, the entire company was only selling $10,000 worth of Stetsine each day. The team I'd build would blast through sales targets, so base pay didn't matter to me at all.

MINDSET:

When I agreed to fly to Arizona for the interviews with Ingrid Biologics, I had the right frame of mind—strategic and deliberate. I wasn't hungry. My heart was in building new opportunities with Frank. By then I'd grown a bit tired of selling pharmaceuticals. Pharmaceutical sales has a great reputation, but it's probably not the best fit for a true sales professional. There are too many contradictions.

Sales drive any organization, but in pharmaceuticals, too many rules and regulations get in the way of the true sales professional. Some companies forbid the sales reps from developing relationships with doctors, which is antithetical to everything written about sales.

I flew out to meet with Ingrid with the idea of qualifying for the role, but not really caring too much if I got it or not. But Ingrid Biologics had something special, and it certainly wasn't the base pay. Nor was it the unlimited cap on commission potential. I had that before with other companies, enabling me to become a top earner.

SELLING: HARD LESSONS LEARNED
Alec Burlakoff/ Training@aburlakoff.com

Ingrid offered something special, and that was in the organizational structure. The other pharmaceutical companies that previously employed me had been a well-established, publicly traded corporations. Early employees that worked for those companies scored big because their compensation packages included large grants of stock options when the companies were still relatively small. By the time I went to work for Magnolia, Stevens & Williams, Excelon, or Argos, grants for stock options were no longer going to the sales team. They could earn bonuses or commissions, but they couldn't ride the huge wave upwards as the company prospered.

Frank was a successful entrepreneur, and I looked forward to developing new projects with him. But in terms of healthcare sales, his company didn't compare. Annual sales would never amount to more than $30 million. Growing bigger would invite complications like corporate boards, venture capital, and regulations or outside oversight that didn't interest him. I saw potential partnership opportunities with Frank, but Ingrid Biologics offered the potential for success on an entirely different level.

For one thing, Jim Shastry had a track record. He started biotech companies previously with successful exits on Wall Street. Early employees would have received grants of stock, or options to purchase stock at pre-market valuation levels. There were only 40 employees at Ingrid Biologics when I went for the interview. And the company hadn't found the right candidate to lead as VP of Sales. If I could maneuver my way into that position, my compensation would include grants of stock that would catapult financial security for our family once Shastry took the company public.

I also knew that I could play a direct role in getting Ingrid Biologics ready for the public markets.

Despite having a new patent with a superior product, the paltry sales at Ingrid opened an awesome opportunity. While at Excelon, I built a sales team and a stable of expert physicians that championed the Excelon product. Stetsine did the same thing, but with its patented spray-delivery system, it was better. I didn't have any doubt that I could call upon my stable of Red doctors. With one phone call, I knew they would stop writing prescriptions for Excelon's product and start writing prescriptions for Stetsine.

In fact, had I been more prudent, I would have shorted stock in Excelon immediately after my meeting with Jim Shastry and Paul Wilson. Because I knew with certainty that they were going to offer me the job of sales manager. And once they saw my results, they'd offer me the position of VP of sales. Sales for Ingrid were about to be *Burlakoffed*. Once that happened, sales for Excelon would take a dump in the marketplace!

SELLING: HARD LESSONS LEARNED
Alec Burlakoff/ Training@aburlakoff.com

Were there red flags when I joined Ingrid Biologics?

Not that I could see at the time. Through the grapevine, I heard that regulators had fined Excelon $400 million because of the ways sales reps were promoting Excelon's drug that treated breakthrough pain for cancer patients. By using practices that I learned and mastered, they succeeded in persuading doctors to prescribe the drug for off-label usage. Yet no one ever spoke with me about having done anything wrong. Instead, I earned rewards and numerous promotions for developing strategies that worked. As far as I could see, we built a successful enterprise at Excelon. The only difference was that I earned commissions for my innovative thinking. Had I joined the company earlier, I would have earned profits.

Ingrid Biologics opened an opportunity for me to earn profits. I sensed an opportunity to finally differentiate myself in the eyes of my father, and my brother Ian. Regardless of how well I had done in any of my previous roles, I never earned the level of income that Ian was earning. When it came to auto sales and the one-call close, Ian was a master-of-the-universe, getting close to $1 million a year in earnings. I looked up to him.

With Ingrid Biologics, I saw an opportunity to change the dynamics. I knew that I could crush sales and play a role in building a publicly traded company. Since I'd be coming in on the ground floor, I'd earn more than commissions. By controlling the tens of thousands of shares in stock, our family's fortunes would rise with the anticipated escalating stock price.

I saw the opportunity of a lifetime, and before I boarded my flight home, I closed what I anticipated was the biggest sale of my life—a job offer at Ingrid Biologics.

CHAPTER 10:
MINDSET AT INGRID

I like the circus. I like to watch performers on death-defying acts, with no safety net. It's thrilling, exhilarating.

When I met with Jim Shastry and Paul Wilson about a sales position at Ingrid, I felt as if I was taking the first steps to cross my own high wire. It would be a position like a circus act of my own. I could see where I was standing, and I could see where I wanted to go. All I had to do was walk across the tight wire. If I balanced everything perfectly, I'd cross over to riches. Unfortunately, I didn't see that by losing my balance, I could fall to my death. There wouldn't be any safety net. What an act!

That is the value that comes with mindset. Do we have the right mindset? Do we have the wrong mindset? Have we identified the values by which we profess to live? Do our goals align with what we say we want to become?

If they do not, we expose ourselves to massive challenge and struggle.

It's crucial for us to check our decision-making process. And as I wrote in the beginning of this project, we can learn such messages from people with whom we cross paths. A Chinese proverb tells us that if you want to know the road ahead, ask someone who is coming back. The Talmud tells us a similar message:

- Peace, peace upon him who is far and him who is near (Isaiah 57:19).

As a Rabbi explained to me, it basically means that the very best teachers in the Jewish religion are actually those who have done wrong in the past. For only those people can teach one the meaning of true redemption.

Redemption begins when we understand where we've been, and how influences led us to the people we've become. We can look at our past decisions and use them to ascertain how we can right our course and get back to moving in the right direction. The alternative is to live with our head in the sand, continuing to make one bad decision after another.

Earlier I used the analogy of an ostrich burying its head in the sand. I wasn't going into this job with Ingrid blindly—I just didn't fully understand the consequences that could follow my decision. When Jim Shastry spoke about his ambitions for Ingrid, he gave off all types of red flags. I didn't have any doubt that risks would come with the position, but I didn't appreciate the magnitude of those risks.

All I saw was a pathway that I had used successfully in every other sales job. I understood the 98/2 rule, and I understood how to connect with physicians. There were wider implications that would not become clear to me until I had gone way too far down the path, and clearly lost my balance.

On the surface, I knew that the FDA approved Stetsine for the management of breakthrough pain in cancer patients. The operative word is cancer patients. During the interview process, Jim Shastry didn't ask what I knew about working with oncologists. Instead, Shastry lasered in on my experience of developing speakers. Specifically, he wanted to know more about my relationships with doctors that specialized in treating pain management.

Instantly, I understood the goal. Dr. Shastry spoke clearly about wanting me to develop an aggressive sales team that would market Stetsine for off-label usage. He didn't even try to masquerade that he wanted me to break the law. Speaking clearly and concisely, he wanted doctors to write more Stetsine in exchange for speaker honorariums.

We both knew that laws wouldn't allow Ingrid to promote off-label usage, but Dr. Shastry wasn't like anyone I'd worked with before. He didn't care about laws. While working at earlier companies, I knew the leaders thought creatively. They wanted reps to promote benefits that pharmaceuticals could provide to all patients. At the same time, they carefully avoided saying anything that could be construed as encouraging reps to recommend drugs for off-label usage.

At Ingrid, Dr. Shastry didn't try to hide his ambitions. He was a beast that I'd never encountered before, and I should have had the good sense to walk away. He didn't see laws applying to his company, and he expected reps to comply with his demands. Regardless of what it would take, Dr. Shastry wanted us to use any means necessary to induce doctors to write more prescriptions for Stetsine.

Specifically, he let me know that:

- A head of sales should develop a stable of physicians to champion Stetsine.

Reps should pay those physicians to become key opinion leaders.

Those physicians should specialize in pain-management, because anyone seeking treatment for pain should be a candidate for Stetsine.

All reps should let the doctors know that if they want to earn more honorariums, they need more "clinical experience" with Stetsine.

SELLING: HARD LESSONS LEARNED
Alec Burlakoff/ Training@aburlakoff.com

To get clinical experience, pain-management physicians would need to write more prescriptions for Stetsine, and write ever-increasing dosage levels.

I didn't bury my head in the sand, and there isn't anyone to blame but myself for sticking around after that meeting. Jim Shastry wanted to blow out sales for Stetsine. He made his goal crystal clear. Rather than promoting the drug to oncologists, he wanted to hire leaders that could think on their feet. He wanted to hire leaders that could craft the sales message in ways to bring results as quickly as possible.

It was a high wire act. It was a circus. I didn't have any doubt that I could cross the high wire and multiply sales levels. As mentioned earlier, when I came on board, Stetsine's pathetic sales volume hovered around $10,000 a day. By using principles that I had honed over the years, I expected to more than 100x those numbers, to more than $1 million in daily sales.

The smart play would've been to grow sales methodically, in a disciplined manner. There were many steps in the sales cycle. It's like there is a wheel, and in order to get the wheel rolling without collapsing, the wheel needed several spokes.

During our interview, I got the sense that Shastry didn't have a full sense of how to develop that sales wheel. He wanted to jump ahead, skipping steps. He wanted to get the wheel rolling without first developing all of the spokes. From Shastry's perspective, building a stable of KOL's would be enough to grow sales. By paying honorariums to physicians, he expected those physicians to champion our drug, providing a return on investment of at least two-to-one. Dr. Shastry said emphatically, "Alec, I want you to pay doctors to prescribe Stetsine." I replied with a cold stone look on my face, I've done it before, I can do it again.

Even more deliberately spoken, if a sales agent authorized a $1,000 honorarium to a physician, Shastry expected that physician to write a minimum of least $2,000 worth of Stetsine. And if the rep were going to pay the physician another honorarium, then the doctor would need to write another $2,000 worth of Stetsine prescriptions. From Dr. Shastry's perspective, a physician should basically become Ingrid's biggest Stetsine advocate, writing as many prescriptions as possible.

The FDA approved Stetsine for breakthrough pain in cancer patients, but oncologists wouldn't have an interest in Stetsine. An oncologist prescribed medication that treated cancer. They wanted to shrink tumors, not lessen pain. If an oncologist's patient suffered from unbearable pain, the oncologist would recommend a pain doctor—if the patient was lucky.

SELLING: HARD LESSONS LEARNED
Alec Burlakoff/ Training@aburlakoff.com

For that reason, Shastry wanted a sales team that specialized in selling to pain-management doctors. The law prohibited him from providing that direction, but he didn't care. He wanted sales leaders to use all their critical-thinking skills. He wanted doctors to prescribe Stetsine to treat any kind of pain, not only breakthrough pain in cancer patients—but *any kind of pain*.

Shastry expected me to execute on his orders. He would hire me as a sales manager, and he dangled the carrot of VP of sales. To seize the opportunity, I would have to engineer a pathway that would lead to more prescriptions of Stetsine. More than anything, I'd need to make sure that the KOLs I developed brought in an ROI of more than two-to-one.

The gambler in me accepted the challenge. I returned to Florida as a sales manager, ready to jump start the sales initiative. First, I coordinated meetings with eight sales reps I inherited. I needed to get an idea of their skills.

Was I working with A players? Or would I need to develop my team?

I contacted each of the sales reps in my region and set up a meeting. We'd start with a breakfast, lunch, or a coffee meeting for a meet and greet. Then, I asked them to set an appointment with their top doctors. I wanted to get in front of those doc-

SELLING: HARD LESSONS LEARNED
Alec Burlakoff/ Training@aburlakoff.com

tors and see how the reps performed. Ideally, those reps would set up dinners where we could have an off-site discussion with physicians on how Stetsine could benefit their practices.

What a disappointment. Within two weeks I'd met with each of the reps. These people hadn't developed any key opinion leaders. Sales had been so slow to get off the ground at Ingrid for a reason. The sales reps didn't understand anything about developing relationships. Like the reps at Argos, they expected literature to sell the product. They didn't grasp that professional, outside sales wasn't about working nine-to-five. The *money hours* were made outside of nine-to-five, on weekends, during dinners, during personal one-on-one time with doctors.

Shastry had given them the resources to grow. But the sales team I inherited didn't have any critical-thinking skills. They didn't have any idea what to do with the tools at their disposal. When I mentioned working weekends or reserving several nights each week to develop relationships with doctors, they looked at me as if I were speaking a foreign language. They didn't understand that before they could sell Stetsine, they would need to learn how to sell themselves. They would need to learn the power of understanding WIFM.

SELLING: HARD LESSONS LEARNED
Alec Burlakoff/ Training@aburlakoff.com

SALES TRAINING:

I felt like taking the bull by the horns and doing the job myself. Within a few days, I knew that I could call upon the stable of Red doctors that I had built over the course of my career. Those doctors knew and understood that if I were calling upon them, they were going to build more efficiencies in their practice. If I couldn't get them closer to what they wanted, they knew I wouldn't be calling upon them at all.

But it wouldn't work for me to step in and do it myself. I was the manager. I needed the sales team to buy into the message I was delivering. I needed them to see and understand how they could build their own wheels, slowly, developing a methodical plan to grow sales and succeed. To do that, I needed a story. I needed the team to learn from an A player, and I knew just the guy to call.

THE BO CRAZEN STORY:

Bo Crazen had been a friend of mine since high school. When I started my career of selling pharmaceuticals for Magnolia, I brought Bo with me. He joined me at Excelon, too. As well as anyone, Bo understood the power of building relationships. By getting the WIFM message, and applying the 98/2 principle, Bo could laser focus on the goal.

And he could blow away expectations with results because of the investments in time that he had made.

When I started my career with Ingrid, Bo was still running sales for Excelon. As I taught during each of my training sessions, Bo understood that developing a professional sales career required us to build each spoke in the wheel. There is an analogy that has become an old cliché in sales. You don't ask a girl to marry you on the first date. Building a relationship takes time, nurturing, and intelligence. If you try to rush the sale along too fast, the relationship will collapse, or fail to get off the ground.

Bo told me the story of how he developed his relationship with Dr. Vi Teng. Along with his colleague, Dr. Teng ran Pain Specialists of Alabama, and he was the co-owner of Greenacres Pharmacy. He was also a classic nerd. As an immigrant from an Asian country, Dr. Teng lived and breathed science. His social life didn't include many friends outside his practice.

Bo Crazen, on the other hand, was a charismatic personality. A former athlete, he stood 6-4 and always had a command presence. Bo lit up any room, and he knew how to use his social magnetism.

"What're you up to this weekend?" Bo said to Dr. Teng on a social call.

"Busy, busy," Dr. Teng told him. He lived in Alabama and he was going to drive a car up to New

York City for his daughter. He intended to make the drive alone, deliver the car, and then fly back to Alabama in time for work on Monday.

"Want some company? I'll be happy to help with the drive and keep it more interesting than if you were to drive alone. Happy to take you to Saphires, my favorite hangout in New York City," Bo told him.

"You'd do that for me, Bo?"

That drive to New York cost Bo a weekend. But it was the start of a relationship with a Red doctor that would pay dividends Bo could reap for life. Bo had a sixth sense for developing such relationships. He knew when to invest the time with a prospective doctor, and he knew when to walk away. He understood the *Burlakoff 98/2 rule*, and that's what made him an A player.

Amateurs would not grasp the power of such relationships without a real-life example. Their visceral reaction would be, "I'm not spending three days in a car with a client. That's not in my job description."

And it's that kind of thinking that limits a sales professional. It doesn't matter whether we're selling pharmaceuticals, diagnostic equipment, medical supplies, or anything else. When it comes to professional sales, it's all about the WIFM, the relationship, and the knowledge of when to invest the time in the right prospect. An A player knows that out of every 100 sales calls, only 2 will be worth the time and energy to deliver top results. An A player knows that he must sell himself before he sells the product.

When I started with Ingrid, I inherited an unimpressive sales team. To jump start their success, I needed a reinforcement. And Bo Crazen was my guy.

To get Bo on my team, I'd have to solve a problem. Bo Crazen was earning a base salary of more than $120,000 plus commissions with his current employer. I knew Bo could solve my problem, but what about his? He wouldn't walk away from a guaranteed salary to join a startup. But to get the results Shastry wanted, I needed an A player that could show our team results.

BREAKING PROTOCOL

The pharmaceutical industry is an ancillary component of the medical profession. As such, it's extremely conservative. Traditionally, the industry only hires full-time employees. They must pass stringent background checks and they must have impeccable credentials, including four-year university degrees. To get the results Shastry wanted, I needed to break that protocol, and I would start with Bo Crazen.

SELLING: HARD LESSONS LEARNED
Alec Burlakoff/ Training@aburlakoff.com

I called Paul Wilson, the CEO and told him my plan. I wanted him to hire Bo Crazen as a 1099 employee. Such a hiring arrangement would be unheard of in pharmaceutical sales. If Bo was so good, Paul asked, why didn't I recruit him to join our sales team?

We need to triage the problem, I explained. I inherited a mediocre sales team that didn't understand how to develop relationships. To deliver on Shastry's expectations of basically buying doctors, I needed everyone on the sales team to learn how to get results. Bo Crazen would get results. We should hire him as a 1099 employee with an extremely limited territory. We could task him to call upon a single doctor. If we brought Crazen on board, sales would start to explode. Those results would spread the Shastry message through the entire company. With the power and speed of a gasoline fire, every salesperson would get the message. Salespeople at Ingrid would finally understand that developing great relationships with doctors leads to explosive sales growth and higher commissions.

Wilson gave me the okay to hire Bo as a 1099 employee. For Bo to earn more money, all he had to do was convince his number-one Red doctor to become a KOL for Stetsine.

Within one week of hiring Bo, he became the number-one sales rep for Ingrid Biologics. In fact, by convincing Dr. Vi Teng to stop writing prescriptions for Excelon, and to start writing prescriptions for Stetsine, the Southeast Region became the number-one region for Ingrid in the country, and it made me the number one manager for Ingrid the first week that I hired Bo.

Those kinds of results were like ringing a bell. As I anticipated, when we reported Bo's sales numbers, his bell woke everyone up.

After we published the results, I coordinated a conference call for our sales team, including Bo. I congratulated Bo on his exceptional performance. Then I asked him to tell the team his secret.

"How did you become the number-one sales rep in the entire company with only one week on the job?"

Bo walked everyone through the importance of building a wheel. He told the story of how he had called upon hundreds of doctors, always searching for the right candidate. Once he found the right candidate, he described how he cultivated the relationship. As a result of that relationship, he had an asset. He could call upon that asset when the time was right. Bo helped Dr. Teng understand how Stetsine could improve his practice. With the drug's patented spray-delivery system, Bo explained that Stetsine would treat patients faster, getting the results for breakthrough pain that they needed.

One of my reps voiced a common objection he heard. "What do you say to a doctor that claims he doesn't have many cancer patients?" The rep worried because the FDA had only approved Stetsine to treat breakthrough pain in cancer patients.

Bo walked him through the simplicity of the objection. Any patient that goes to see a pain-management doctor suffers. Those patients were already taking medication in accordance with a scheduled pain-management regimen. Bo said he would point to the doctor that there would not be a single patient in his practice that did not—at some point—suffer from breakthrough pain. It was uncontrollable. The patient may keel over and feel excruciating pain. He couldn't get off the floor. In his mind, the only solution would be a trip to the emergency room.

"I'd help the doctor understand how Stetsine would be like giving the patient the equivalent of an emergency room that he could carry in his pocket. If he ever suffered from breakthrough pain, one spray of Stetsine beneath the tongue and the pain disappears immediately."

Bo said he wouldn't directly tell a doctor to prescribe Stetsine off label. But he would help the doctor see how any patient that suffered from breakthrough pain would benefit from a Stetsine prescription. The doctor would benefit because the patient would be grateful. And insurance companies may even be grateful, because it would save them money that they would otherwise have to pay hospitals for emergency room visits.

It was that process that led Bo to convert his number-one Red doctor into a KOL for Stetsine. And to be a KOL for Stetsine, the doctor needed more clinical experience with Stetsine. How did he get that clinical experience? By writing more Stetsine prescriptions.

Bo knew how to build every spoke in the wheel. First, he found his Red doctor. Then, he nurtured a relationship with his Red doctor, investing time and energy as necessary, regardless of work hours. Once he had that relationship, he would develop the doctor as a speaker, making him a Key Opinion Leader. That way, he could ensure his return on investment. Certainly, the honorarium was an important spoke in the sales wheel that Bo built. It may have been the most important spoke. Still, without all of the other spokes, the wheel would collapse.

Bringing Bo on board was like bringing a shot of ether to a carburetor. As a 1099 employee, he was on track to earn an extra $500,000 annually from commissions at Ingrid. More importantly, he helped me show others how to grow into an A player. Other members of my team started to fall in line, and soon I had two A players out of eight.

Within three months, I accepted the offer to become VP of sales for Ingrid Biologics. But just before making the move to Arizona, I found another opportunity to accelerate sales by breaking protocol.

CHAPTER 11:
COLLAPSING THE WHEEL

As I anticipated, sales at Ingrid Biologics exploded in the Southeast Region within weeks of my joining the company. We succeeded as a result of the extensive list of Red doctors that Bo and I had carefully created over time. Relationships—for all sales professional—are invaluable assets. If cultivated correctly, they're renewable resources that a sales pro can tap again and again for mutually beneficial reasons.

Anyone that wants to build a career in professional sales needs to grasp the importance of nurturing relationships.

If the sales professional knows and fully understands the customer's business model, the sales professional can always bring the customer opportunities to increase efficiencies and build more value.

When the sales professional brings more value to the customer, the professional earns higher earnings.

By nurturing relationships properly, both parties in the relationship benefit. We squander opportunities if we don't make use of this key aspect of sales.

SELLING: HARD LESSONS LEARNED
Alec Burlakoff/ Training@aburlakoff.com

When I accepted responsibilities as an area manager for the Southeast region, there wasn't a single sales rep on the team that had any idea on how to develop powerful, mutually beneficial relationships. And from what I could gather, reps in other regions didn't have much experience in building relationships, either.

Shastry didn't make it easy. By offering a base salary that was about half of what other pharmaceutical companies offered to reps, stars like Bo were not interested in applying at Ingrid.

Since we needed more stars like Bo, I'd have to either recruit or train new hires for the other regions. They had to understand the concept of Time / Access / Interest.

We needed reps that knew how to spend their time wisely. Rather than focusing on doctors that wouldn't listen, they had to develop filters to identify doctors that would be most likely to grow with them.

We needed reps that could create access to the doctors. Rather than allowing the doctor's gatekeepers to waste their time, they would know how to meet the doctors on their terms, in accordance with their timelines.

We needed reps that could cultivate an interest in the doctor, making him want to listen. If the doctor showed a willingness to learn how and why our product could improve his practice, a sales rep could bring more value.

When Jim Shastry promoted me to Vice President of Sales, I had a responsibility to build and train a new team. They would have to develop the right kind of relationships with the right kind of doctors. They needed to know the formula described above:

- Time / Access / Interest.

Seems simple enough. In reality, few people grasped the power of this recipe. And once given the recipe, few sales professionals knew how to really use the recipe as effectively as Bo.

Sales is a combination of art and science. Those who developed the highest level of skill would succeed at the highest levels. Those who wanted to measure the number of hours worked, emails sent, or calls made would never be more than B-players. They wouldn't last long on our sales team.

Shastry expected me to grow sales for Stetsine in every region of the country as quickly as possible. Yet he didn't appreciate the magnitude of this task. Growing sales required engineering, planning, methodical steps and commitment. And we had to take into account all of the company's strengths and weaknesses, a concept that seemed foreign to Shastry.

SELLING: HARD LESSONS LEARNED
Alec Burlakoff/ Training@aburlakoff.com

Ingrid Biologics may have had the strength of a superior delivery system with its patented spray technology. Yet the company also had weaknesses. As a new medication on the market, Stetsine lacked the name recognition and backing of established pharmaceutical companies like Excelon. Sales professionals would view the Ingrid compensation package that offered unlimited commission earnings as a strength, but the paltry base pay would make it difficult to attract sales professionals that had already developed relationships with a stable of Red doctors.

I had to balance these strengths and weaknesses while crossing the high wire at Ingrid, knowing there was no safety net beneath me. Either we would succeed together as a company, or I would fail as a VP of sales.

In reality, as professionals we're constantly faced with such dilemmas. We have choices, and it's up to us to make the right choice. For that reason, we should always consult our moral compass, our code of values. By making decisions that align with what is most important in our life, we are better able to choose the right course of action.

At Ingrid, I lost sight of the right course of action. Rather than considering the implications of all my decisions, I compromised, delivering what Shastry demanded of me rather than making the right decisions. I built a team that would explode sales for Stetsine, even though I saw red flags all around me.

THE FORMULA: TIME / ACCESS / INTEREST:

Anyone that could follow the formula could succeed in sales. It's like adhering to the recipe for baking a cake. A recipe told us precisely what ingredients we needed and what specific measurements to use. A recipe told us how hot to preheat the oven, and how long to bake the cake. If we followed the recipe, we got what we wanted. If we added extra ingredients, or skipped some ingredients, or didn't follow the precise order, we would get something entirely different. To get what we wanted, we had to follow the recipe and sequence precisely.

In sales, we had to do the same. We had to allocate our time wisely, using the 98/2 rule. We needed to access our doctors on their terms, where they would give us their attention. If they had an interest in learning how we could benefit their practice, we had to do everything possible to nurture, grow, and strengthen/reinforce the relationship.

We couldn't cut corners with expectations of speeding things along. Cutting corners in sales equated to a baker that would try to speed up the process. He couldn't bake at twice the temperature and expect to get the cake in half the time. Likewise, in sales we had to follow the formula precisely if we wanted to get the right results.

Given Shastry's unreasonable demands and expectations for growth, I had to think creatively every day. Shastry wanted sales and he wanted them immediately. To deliver, I put every manager on notice that I'd measure productivity, *not activity*. Some of the area managers I inherited had to go.

Molly, the area manager for our mid-Atlantic region, wasn't going to work out. She led a sales team that covered Michigan, Illinois, Indiana, Wisconsin, and other states around the Great Lakes. Molly liked to stay busy. Her emails were 10 pages long. She took pride authoring training manuals that covered all the mechanisms of action for Stetsine. Her sales team got logistical guidance, with maps and instructions on how frequently they should call upon doctors located in a specific area.

Somehow, Molly didn't grasp her role as a sales leader. Success would only come from productivity, not clerical charts or tracking employee activities. Under my watch, we would measure productivity by bringing in new revenues. Since she couldn't get the job done, she had to go. And I found the right person to put in her place, at least I thought so at the time.

SELLING: HARD LESSONS LEARNED
Alec Burlakoff/ Training@aburlakoff.com

BRANDI:

Before moving my family from Florida to Arizona to transition into my new role as VP of sales, I broke corporate protocol. As I wrote previously, to its core, the pharmaceutical industry is conservative. It puts job candidates through rigorous background checks. Before hiring anyone, pharmaceutical companies required universities to send sealed transcripts, confirming that a prospective employee had earned excellent grades and a four-year degree, masters and doctoral degree preferred.

In my career as a sales professional, I was either directly or indirectly responsible for selling more than $3 billion worth of pharmaceutical medications. Experience convinced me that excelling in sales didn't require college. That's not to say that I have anything against formal education. Prior to my career in sales, I invested the time to earn a bachelor's degree and a master's degree. But pieces of paper didn't move the needle when it came to sales.

Anyone could become a great sales professional if that person learned how to build every spoke in the wheel. If a person could nurture relationships, understand the WIFM, learn how to focus on the best prospects, show the prospect how to create more value, that person could become a star. Some people that didn't finish high school knew how to sell instinctively, while some people that had advanced degrees, like Molly, got too caught up in minutiae, blocking their ability to sell.

Sales drove everything. And Brandi understood how to break down barriers, build relationships, and get the order. Despite natural gifts that would make her an excellent salesperson, she didn't have a university degree. In fact, I doubt whether Brandi graduated from high school.

Ordinarily, Brandi's lack of credentials wouldn't result in an interview with a pharmaceutical company. I met her accidentally, while at a strip club in Florida. Don't judge! Remember, as sales professionals, we meet our clients on their schedule, making it easy for them. One of my Red doctors and I had dinner at a club of his choice. When we were ready to leave, the waitress discovered that she had mistakenly given my credit card to another customer. After apologizing, the waitress said that she already called him and he was on his way back to fix the mix up at the club, exchanging my card for his.

No problem. The doctor and I said our goodbyes and I sat down at a common area table to wait. I'd never met Brandi before, but she walked over and asked if I wanted company.

I didn't want to waste her time. She was working. Without a credit card I didn't have money to buy drinks or anything else. I told her about the mix up and that I'd be leaving as soon as the guy returned my card.

"That's okay," she said. "I'll keep you company while you wait."

She conversed easily. Without trying, she showed an interest in my career and spoke openly about hers. When I asked how she got into her line of work, she didn't hesitate. She told me about a difficult childhood and how she emancipated herself at 16. Since then, she'd been on her own, surviving, growing, learning how to create opportunities out of nothing. By the time the guy returned my card, we'd spoken for 30 minutes. All I could think about was what a great sales manager she'd make.

"You're in the wrong business," I told her before leaving. "You should be in professional sales. You've got a natural gift for disarming people, understanding them, and opening them up to listen."

Brandi expressed interest and confidence. If a professional sales organization would hire her, she pledged to do anything and everything to become a top earner. Attitude made all the difference, and she had the right attitude.

"Here's your once-in-a-lifetime chance to change your career path." I offered to meet Brandi the following day at a coffee shop. "Wear your best business attire. Convince me that you can fit into a professional sales environment. If you can do that, I'll teach you the rest."

Brandi didn't have a resume or university transcripts, but I didn't have any doubt that she could sell. Fortunately, at Ingrid Biologics, I knew that I could break protocol. I could point to how well it worked out when we hired Bo as a 1099 employee. Putting my name and reputation on the line, I pledged that neither Brandi's lack of educational credentials nor her lack of experience would interfere with her becoming a sales star.

And within weeks of hiring her to become the area sales manager for the mid-Atlantic region, Brandi crushed expectations. How did she do it? She followed the exact recipe that anyone else could have followed.

She scheduled a meet and greet with the ten sales reps that would report to her.

She asked her sales reps to schedule office visits with their top-prescribing doctors.

She accompanied her sales reps on the office visits and identified the doctors that would be most receptive to listening to her message.

Her reconnaissance mission led her to Dr. Andrews, who owned one of the most successful pain-management practices in Chicago. With a stream of referrals from oncologists, neurologists, and primary-care doctors, Dr. Andrews' clinics treated more than 150 patients every day.

By building rapport with Dr. Andrews, Brandi could deliver her message. Overall, he had more than 10,000 patients in his practice, and all of them suffered at one time or another from breakthrough pain. As a result of her building each spoke in the wheel, Dr. Andrews willingly listened as Brandi explained the drug's mechanisms of action. Stetsine could be a powerful medication for patients in his practice, and if he developed more clinical experience with the drug, he would see all the ways that it benefited patients. The FDA approved Stetsine for breakthrough pain in cancer patients because during the clinical trials, it was tested on Cancer patients. But clinical experience would show that Stetsine could help patients suffering from any kind of breakthrough pain. They'd get a better quality of life if they could respond immediately with Stetsine.

Brandi developed Dr. Andrews into a key opinion leader, and he championed Stetsine at dinners she coordinated. She had the budget to pay his honorariums, but by writing more prescriptions, he brought a seven-to-one return on investment. Shastry was more than happy; he was enamored!

Dr. Andrews prescribed Stetsine to more patients. He happily received honorariums in exchange for attending more dinners. Brandi listened and made Dr. Andrews feel important. She gave him what he most needed, slowly but surely becoming his best friend.

Stetsine allowed him to grow his practice by treating patients that needed pain management most—not only cancer patients, but any patient that suffered from breakthrough pain.

By following each step in the formula, Brandi developed a whale within weeks on the job. Others envied her success. Since they didn't follow the formula precisely, few other sales reps were able to get the job done. Instead of developing doctors into key opinion leaders, using the precise formula that we taught, amateurs bluntly offered the doctors cash to write prescriptions. I had to fire several sales reps for cutting corners.

Building a successful career in professional sales required the critical thinking skills to nurture relationships carefully. It's not about the hours a person puts in, but about the way a person thinks. And college didn't teach those skills on mindset. Brandi may not have had Molly's academic pedigree, but she had the mindset of a sales professional.

ARIZONA:

As VP of sales, I invested countless hours to help reps grasp the importance of going through every step in the sale cycle. We had to operate as professionals, delivering a high quality of service to the right doctors. And we had to stay on the job until we reached our goals.

To teach this message, I shared stories about my father, an outstanding car salesman. People took a perverse pleasure in ridiculing car salesmen, but they're some of the hardest working people I know. I learned more about sales from my dad and brother than from anyone else. Their work ethic inspired me.

Unlike pharmaceutical sales, a car salesman had to do or die. He didn't get a base salary, an expense account, or any of the perks that we took for granted in professional sales. If my dad didn't succeed in his role, he didn't eat. And he knew how to define success. He didn't need a manger to tell him what to do. If he didn't sell a car during his 8:00 am to 3:00 pm shift, he'd work the second shift, staying on the lot until 9:00 pm.

We needed that same spirit on the sales team at Ingrid. Reps like Bo and Brandi got it, but most did not.

I spoke openly about expectations. Every sales professional should use his or her critical thinking skills to develop five Key Opinion Leaders. They should have five more Key Opinion Leaders on the bench, ready to step in and fill the gap if anyone fell off. If a sales pro followed the formula I taught, that strategy should yield at least one physician writing at least one new prescription for Stetsine every day.

Those results would prepare our company to go public, generating millions of dollars in liquidity for Shastry and the rest of the leadership team at Ingrid—including me. The allure of wealth from stock options I received as part of my compensation clouded my judgment. Ignoring red flags, I kept pushing ahead to comply with Shastry's demands for higher sales. I knew that sales volumes would drive the stock price higher, and I built a team that could deliver.

By the time I cultivated my team at Ingrid, we boosted sales to more than 300 new daily prescriptions. Taken together, new sales plus existing orders put us on track to generate more than $3 million in daily sales—more than $1 billion in annual revenues. Wall Street rewarded our apparent success, raising the value of our stock so it would become the most successful IPO in 2013.

SHORT SIGHTED SUCCESS:

When I started at Ingrid Biologics, I didn't intend to build a long-term career. Changes in the sleep-diagnostics industry influenced my decision to take the job. At Ingrid, I saw an opportunity I could seize to supplement my income.

When Shastry and Wilson dangled stock options, I went all in. An allocation of pre-IPO stock put my interests in line with Shastry and the rest of the leadership team; it also blinded my sense of propriety. When I saw corporate wrongdoing, I turned the other way. Instead of thinking about the implications of my decisions, I considered the short-term rewards.

For years I'd been trying to earn an income that would be high enough to feel as if I was worthy. I'd been measuring myself by money ever since I heard that snide comment from the guy in the Bentley at the Ridge Pines School. At Ingrid, I wouldn't only be earning a salary and commissions. My wealth would rise with the company's stock price, and the company's stock price would rise as long as our team kept bringing in the sales.

THE REIMBURSEMENT CHARADE:

Our team proved that it could generate sales for Stetsine. But sales were only one part of the equation. Insurance companies still had to pay for the prescriptions. From my work at Excelon, I understood industry standards. Typically, insurance companies authorized payment for about 20% of the prescriptions for drugs that competed with Stetsine. Despite those standards, Shastry expected insurance companies to pay for 90% of Stetsine prescriptions that doctors wrote.

Shastry's expectations were not only unreasonable, they were absurd. Greed drove his decisions, and he launched a billing scheme to manipulate and deceive insurance companies into paying for more Stetsine prescriptions. He wasn't about to let insurance companies interfere with growth targets. If our sales team got doctors to write prescriptions, Shastry made sure that another team brought the support. They would complete the cycle by getting insurance companies to pay.

Although doctors had discretion to write prescriptions for off-label usage of Stetsine, insurance companies would only pay approved usage. They would pay for Stetsine if the patient had a cancer diagnosis and suffered from breakthrough pain. If the patient didn't have cancer, few insurance companies would even consider paying.

To get around this obstacle, Shastry created a Stetsine prior authorization service and he offered it as a perk for physicians. Rather than wasting time arguing with insurance companies for payment, doctors could outsource the task of obtaining authorizations to us. Ostensibly, our so called "reimbursement specialists" would take care of everything, providing a real benefit to doctors and their staff.

In reality, the billing service Shastry authorized deceived insurance companies. Telemarketers would call the insurance companies, masquerading as if they were actually employed by the doctor's office. They knew specifically what to say in order to get a prior authorization for the prescription. The telemarketer would say anything necessary to get the insurance company to authorize payment for the prescription, including lying by saying the patient suffered from cancer.

Despite knowing that Shastry had orchestrated a billing fraud, I went along.

For the bad decisions I've made, I'll be paying a heavy price for life.

CHAPTER 12:
LESSONS LEARNED

At this stage in my life, I like to paraphrase Henry Ford, who once said:

- Failure is simply the opportunity to begin again, this time more intelligently than the time before.

After devoting two decades as a professional sales representative in healthcare, I'm beginning again—largely because I didn't make values-based, goal-oriented decisions from the start. That's a lesson I'll never forget. Anyone beginning a career in sales or business would be wise to learn from failure.

Bad decisions give us intelligence. If we don't use that intelligence to grow, then it's no one's fault but our own if we fail again. At any given time, we can pause, reflect, figure out what we've done right, what we've done wrong, and what we're going to do with the rest of the time we have remaining.

Besides reflecting on our own decisions, we should think about what we see around us.

How have others made decisions?

SELLING: HARD LESSONS LEARNED
Alec Burlakoff/ Training@aburlakoff.com

In what ways have those decisions led people down a pathway to success?

What failures have they learned along the way?

What can we do differently with our life, in light of what we're learning?

Life is short. It may not feel that way when we're 20 or 30. Once we reach our 40s, we can look back and think with the benefit of hindsight. What have we done and what would we like to do differently? If we use that intelligence to make better decisions, we change the trajectory of our life.

In retrospect, there were many times when I should have used intelligence and values-based, goal-oriented tactics to make the best decisions. Others should do the same.

When I left my role as an educator and guidance counselor at The Ridge Pines School, I made the right decision. Stephanie and I were bringing our first child into the world. I prioritized family. A wicked parent demoralized me, making it clear that I couldn't continue working in education. "Petty rules, from petty people," he told me. His statement didn't align with how I saw myself. Nevertheless, I walked away knowing that I had to make a change. If I didn't put myself in a position to earn more money, I would not be able to provide for Stephanie and our daughter the way I wanted. I had to pursue a different path. At that moment, I couldn't feel great about my career in education.

When an opportunity opened to join the pharmaceutical industry, I seized the initiative, doing everything within my power to make the change. The potential to triple my salary guided my decision to go all in. Along the way, I had to make choices. What could I learn from the choices I made?

What could you learn from the choices I made?

These questions should always guide us. By asking good questions, assessing our options, we can steer clear of disaster.

During my career, there were many times when I focused on the sale, ignoring a personal responsibility to make such assessments. That's the dilemma of every salesperson. Blind loyalty to the client can lead us to the top of our profession. But if we we're willfully blind to ethical standards and the principles of good character, our success may have a short lifespan. In my case, "loyalty to the sale" had devastating results, influencing the lives of people I love, and millions of people I will never know.

As I reflect, I see the collateral fallout. By ignoring all the warning signs around me, I made it possible for an opioid epidemic to spread. Character flaws did not occur to me while I was in the heat of the sale, and heavy costs ensued.

SELLING: HARD LESSONS LEARNED
Alec Burlakoff/ Training@aburlakoff.com

If I applied the same color code that I used to assess prospective doctors, I was a pure-Red sales professional. There wasn't anything in my life or the choices that I made that resembled the amiability of a Yellow, or the environmentalism of a Green. If the conversation wasn't about sales, I didn't have any interest. There could be a little Blue in me, as I could be scientific, but only if discussing case studies and mechanisms of action on the medications I sold would help me close a deal.

At my core, I was Red, all business. As an old saying in sales goes, *I'd eat a shit sandwich to close a deal with the right client.* Loyalty to the art and science of sales governed all my decisions.

In retrospect, I see ancillary consequences from decisions I made. Whereas values and goals *should* have guided my decisions, I trained my mind to focus on what would get the deal done. Such a mindset resulted in crushing sales targets. Yet by ignoring values and goals, I embraced a strategy that equated to winning a race that resulted in a fatal crash when I hit the finish line. We've got to think about the broader implications of our decisions, the opportunities and threats that accompany choices we make.

Such tactics of critical thinking elude us when we ignore ethics, morality, and the spirit of the law. Choices I made influenced our community and the lives of people I love.

SELLING: HARD LESSONS LEARNED
Alec Burlakoff/ Training@aburlakoff.com

By focusing on short-term goals, we may not see the wider implications of our decisions. Earlier in this manuscript, I wrote about Marcus Aurelius. As an exercise to strengthen his decision-making skills, he invested thousands of hours to write out his thoughts in his book, *Meditations*. Similarly, a Rabbi helped me grasp the ripple effect of every decision. The best way to make better decisions in the future is to learn from past decisions, to internalize how past decisions led to our current situation.

While writing about my journey to become a sales leader, I frequently described the qualities I wanted to see in members of my team. A great salesperson would need to identify, quickly, the value of time. By not understanding the 98/2 rule, that salesperson would never reach the highest level. If a doctor took the time to listen to us, showed interest in our product, and granted us access to reach him, he would become a part of our 2% club, getting 98% of our attention. Experience convinces me that such strategies lead to exceptional performance in sales.

Yet exceptional performance in sales does not free us from responsibility. In my case, my priority was being a husband, a father, and a citizen. Unfortunately, my actions didn't support the values by which I professed to live. Decisions I made suggested that my role as a sales leader for Ingrid was my highest priority.

SELLING: HARD LESSONS LEARNED
Alec Burlakoff/ Training@aburlakoff.com

Every decision we make comes with an opportunity cost. We don't always see those costs, but we can always improve. Since I've gone through the crossroads and paid the price for my decisions, I see more clearly. All along the journey I could have paused, assessed, and gotten myself on track to reach the goals that I set for my life. I didn't. That self-assessment and reflection should be a part of our professional development.

Anywhere in society, with people young and old, we see examples of men and women who make decisions without thinking of the long-term implications. Their decisions may not break laws, but they can certainly lead to personal struggle. Media reports abound with stories of people in their 40s, 50s, 60s, and 70s that did not put plans in place to prepare for retirement. On the other end of the spectrum, we see how a crisis with crippling student loan debt has complicated the future for an entire generation of young people.

For the past decade, millions of students have taken on loans to pay tuition bills. A high percentage of those students quit before finishing, or they pursue jobs after graduation that didn't have anything to do with their academic credentials. Asking good questions may have helped them make better decisions before they took on the debt.

Anyone can ask:

- How am I defining success in my life?
- What options exist?
- How will the choices I make align with who and what I want to become in five years, or ten years?
- What goals am I setting that will take me from where I am to where I want to go?
- What level of commitment am I willing to make to succeed?
- Are all of my decisions aligning with how I'm defining success?
- How am I holding myself accountable?
- What level of awareness do I have regarding opportunities that align with my values?

Asking those kinds of questions is an art and a science. They can help us develop our careers in ways that allow us to evolve as human beings. Good decision making starts with identifying our values, then asking good questions that help us find a path that lead to our success. Our decisions should harmonize with the values by which we profess to live.

Bad decisions led me into the crosshairs of the criminal justice system. There are lessons in that

SELLING: HARD LESSONS LEARNED
Alec Burlakoff/ Training@aburlakoff.com

failure. I've learned from them, and others can learn as well.

FALLOUT FROM INGRID:

When I agreed to join the sales team at Ingrid, I felt as if my life was in turmoil. Economics in the sleep-study industry had changed, leaving me with feelings of vulnerability. With insurers paying less for the services we offered, it would only be a matter of time before my compensation would suffer. When the opportunity opened at Ingrid, I seized it, knowing that I had the experience, skillset, and resources to build a sales organization. I felt as if I could do the job in my sleep.

As a professional sales leader, I knew precisely how I would grow a sales team for Stetsine, the product Ingrid wanted me to sell. With sales, it's all about human-to-human interaction, regardless of what we're selling. While training others, I'd help them understand key principles:

- Identify the clients most likely to work with you
- Determine the level of access that the prospective client would offer
- Devote 98% attention to 2% of the clients

- Always articulate how the prospective client would benefit

Whether it's business-to-business sales, business-to-consumer sales, or business-to-government sales, it's all about human-to-human connectivity. If we know how to connect with others, we bring value. I knew that I could create a team that would bring value to any product I sold. With the Ingrid products, I had both experience and an edge because of relationships I had built with doctors over decades.

As a sales professional, I always emphasized the importance of making a human connection. How do we connect? We connect by listening. We connect by wanting to learn more about the problems our customers want to solve. We connect through loyalty and getting the customer to say yes. That's what human-to-human sales are all about, and it doesn't take a university degree to get that human connection.

On the other hand, regardless of how good we become at making those human-to-human connections, if we don't align our decisions with our values, we set ourselves up for failure. Sometimes, that failure comes on a massive scale.

SELLING: HARD LESSONS LEARNED
Alec Burlakoff/ Training@aburlakoff.com

IGNORING WARNING SIGNS:

At Ingrid, I didn't align decisions with my values. Characteristically, I was all Red. I adhered to the principles of professional sales, ignoring responsibilities of good citizenship. The FDA approved Stetsine for a specific purpose: as breakthrough pain medication for cancer patients. Yet Jim Shastry, the CEO at Ingrid, wanted to grow sales by any means necessary. He wanted doctors prescribing Stetsine for *every* type of pain. If a person had a troublesome hangnail, Shastry considered Stetsine a viable remedy. When insurance companies balked at paying for off-label prescriptions of Stetsine, Shastry and his team created a reimbursement charade to get around those troubles.

As head of sales, I didn't have access to internal dialogues between Ingrid's Chairman, CEO, and attorneys. They didn't want me to know that regulators were questioning the Ingrid legal team about our sales practices. Instead, they wanted me marching full-steam ahead, motivating our sales team to grow, grow, grow.

Despite there being warning signs, I didn't question them. I was willfully blind, failing my family, my community, and my profession. I had personal reasons to ignore the red flags:

- My compensation was directly tied to sales growth.

- My compensation included stock options that would become more valuable as the company's stock price increased.
- Rules only allowed executives to sell stock in relatively small increments each month, meaning that I had to keep the momentum going so that I could convert my stock into cash.
- My earnings had a direct influence on my self-esteem.

In retrospect, I see how all of those factors influenced me to ignore warning signs. As a direct result of my performance as a sales leader, Ingrid became the best-performing stock of all new companies for the year. The flipside was that I also had a direct role in fueling an opioid epidemic across the United States.

Leaders at our company didn't reveal that regulators were investigating our company because they didn't want anything to disrupt sales. As the sales leader, my marching orders came from the highest level. The chairman of the company put the pressure on, demanding daily feedback. If a sales rep failed to meet his unrealistically high sales quotas, he ordered me to fire that rep or face termination myself.

SELLING: HARD LESSONS LEARNED
Alec Burlakoff / Training@aburlakoff.com

WHITE COLLAR CRIME

Although I tried to ignore the signs, I didn't want to walk away until I cashed out all of my stock. As a result, I played a key role in a criminal conspiracy. At one point, the general counsel at Ingrid informed several people on the sales team—including me—that the company had hired an outside lawyer. Theoretically, the lawyer was supposed to represent us and be available for any questions we may have had about our business practices. We were told that he was a civil lawyer, and that we should direct questions to him if we were concerned about our sales tactics.

I didn't see any value in consulting with that lawyer. Instead, I kept selling.

When a company hires a lawyer to represent members of the sales force, it's a good sign that something isn't going well. There's an acronym for it:

- CYA—Cover Your Ass.

The company wanted to protect itself, building plausible deniability and separating itself from the sales engine that kept the company growing. Rather than digging for answers on why the company hired a lawyer, I soldiered on, continuing to drive the sales force so that they would exceed expectations.

SELLING: HARD LESSONS LEARNED
Alec Burlakoff/ Training@aburlakoff.com

Experts in white collar crime have a theory that they call the Fraud Triangle. According to this theory, when three points link up, they influence possibilities for criminal behavior:

- The person feels pressure of some sort, as if he has to generate more money.
- The person sees an opportunity to leverage his position to generate more money.
- The person rationalizes that his behavior isn't really a crime.

As I read about this so-called "fraud triangle," I identified with the explanation. There is no excuse for the lines that I crossed. But as I look back, I know that I felt enormous pressure. I wanted to measure up to the earning power of my father and my brother. As VP of sales, I had the discretion to influence sales. By selling as much Stetsine as possible, the company's stock price would continue to rise. I could rationalize that our team only told the doctor the different ways that Stetsine could benefit his patients. Since the doctor would write the prescription, our sales team wasn't really doing anything wrong.

Pressure, opportunity, and rationalization.

Despite my leadership role in the company, I didn't see myself as a criminal at the time. If anyone had invited me to join a criminal enterprise, I would have thought the suggestion ludicrous. But I ignored all kinds of signs that, if I had been making values-based decisions, would have led me to walk away. Even when leaders at the company created a reimbursement center to manipulate insurance companies into paying for off-label prescriptions, I stuck with it. Warped thinking resulted in criminal charges for all leaders of the company, including me.

NEXT STEPS:

Life is about assessing where we are and assessing where we're going. The fallout from my career decisions has been enormous for our society. More personally, I've seen the toll that my failures have brought to the people I love. I became a scapegoat of my company, resulting in my name being tarnished in the national media. More than $9 million in anticipated compensation vanished overnight. Both civil and criminal proceedings have complicated my life for years, making it impossible for me to advance.

Despite those complications, I accept full responsibility for architecting the next chapter of my life. Every day, I pick myself up and give 100 percent effort to making things right.

It's never too early, and it's never too late to start moving in the right direction. And the right direction begins with an understanding that I have to deal with the fallout, that I have to deal with the world that I created, as it exists and not as how I want it to be.

And how will I succeed going forward?

Traditional employment opportunities may be limited as a consequence of my past, but I'm determined to go forward living a life of meaning and relevance. I am pausing, I am assessing, and I am making values-based, goal-oriented decisions. I learned that the right decision at the wrong time is the wrong decision.

Rather than rushing in to the next venture, I'm reflecting on the decisions I made that got me here. I'm anticipating where I want to be in five years and ten years, considering the various options that will take me there. When contemplating my options, I consider opportunity costs, knowing that every decision puts me on a path—ensuring that I'm on the *right* path is my responsibility.

Despite making some bad decisions, I built and trained sales teams that generated more than $3 billion in revenues. The true sales professional builds trust and authenticity with people that want to say no. Becoming a best-in-class sales professional requires training in how to stay positive and motivated, even when dealing with objections or rejection.

SELLING: HARD LESSONS LEARNED
Alec Burlakoff/ Training@aburlakoff.com

Courses I now create teach *Burlakoff's Rules of Success*, while simultaneously showing the pitfalls that can lead to failure. With video files, audio files, and lesson plans, this training teaches sales pros how to reach the highest levels, while simultaneously avoiding catastrophes with personal compliance and accountability training.

Hope to see you in the course!

FINAL CHAPTER
EPILOGUE

In January 2020, a federal judge sentenced me to serve 26 months for my role in the Ingrid affair. The sentence could have been much longer, but I certainly hoped for something shorter.

I didn't know what would come from serving time in federal prison, and I didn't know what to expect. How does a person prepare for the trauma of being ripped away from family and community?

In truth, I didn't know.

Since switching careers from teaching to sales, I morphed into a triple-A personality, eager to do anything to close a deal. For decades, I lived with the delusion that I'd been an outstanding corporate player, building relationships that advanced the agenda for my employers. They rewarded performance, feeding delusions that by bringing in more sales, I excelled at my job.

Now, in retrospect, I recognize that—despite being a sales professional—I had a higher duty. As an American citizen, I also had to abide by the social contract. In exchange for the privilege of living in this great country, each of us has a duty to abide by the law.

SELLING: HARD LESSONS LEARNED
Alec Burlakoff/ Training@aburlakoff.com

There isn't anything inherently wrong with the tactic of cultivating relationships, or even the 98/2 rule that I developed. In fact, I would still argue that a sales professional may do well by focusing 98% attention on the 2% of qualified leads that express interest; people may not take time to listen to a sales pitch, but they'll always make time to spend with their friends. Nevertheless, if we're improperly inducing those prospects with unethical incentives, we begin eroding and sliding down a path that can lead to problems. The honorarium payments I authorized and encouraged for Red Doctors, and the reimbursement charade my employer concocted, led to my being complicit in criminal activities.

When my employer urged me to grow sales by anything necessary, I should have given my honest services. By then, however, I'd become all-too familiar with the WIFM tactics that I'd honed over the years. I fought hard to recruit my man Bo Crazen because I recognized him as a master of the manipulation game. The tactic worked in the short term. Our sales grew quickly, and the market rewarded us with a multi-billion-dollar valuation. Yet in the end, our tactics disgraced the system and victimized people. In the end, it cost shareholders billions, contributed to other problems for people I didn't even know, and brought collateral consequences for people I loved. The fallout would send my reputation into tatters.

SELLING: HARD LESSONS LEARNED
Alec Burlakoff/ Training@aburlakoff.com

When authorities began investigating our business practices, and they targeted me for prosecution, I went through these weird mental stages, starting with denial, clinging to beliefs that I could talk my way out of the problems I created. The longer the proceedings carried on, the more I felt myself deflating, with energy leaving me every day. I couldn't muster the strength to get going. The couch—and staring at the wall—became my therapy.

Introspection helped me to break away from that catatonic state of self-loathing for the opportunities I squandered:

- How did I get here?
- What drove me into this mess?
- Why did this happen?

The more I contemplated those questions, the deeper I sunk into despondency. I had to ask a different series of questions:

- What steps can I take today to begin moving forward?
- How can I take lessons from my past to build a new life?

- In what ways can I reconcile with society for the damage I've caused?

Those questions helped me imagine something better. I needed to get on with the next chapter, because the alternative would be to drop further into a debilitating despondency. If I could stop dwelling on my bad decisions, I could architect a plan to reconcile. I would need to begin creating and making amends. Writing this story felt like a step in the right direction. It helped me to accept responsibility, to acknowledge that where I had gone wrong, and to think differently. The exercise in personal development proved incredibly therapeutic.

> "We must be before we can do, and we can do only to the extent which we are, and what we are depends upon what we think."
> —Charles F. Hannel

Those words of Charles Hannel, an American entrepreneur and writer, inspired me. He helped me to quit feeling sorry for myself and start writing a new chapter. Then I had to write the next chapter. Before I could write the final chapter, I had to climb through the 26-month prison term that my judge imposed.

SELLING: HARD LESSONS LEARNED
Alec Burlakoff/ Training@aburlakoff.com

Life, as it turns out, is always about incremental steps.

In early 2020, after the judge imposed my term, the Bureau of Prisons ordered me to surrender to a federal prison in Miami. At the same time, COVID had been wreaking havoc across the country, and on the world, disrupting life as we knew it. For the first time in generations, governments began issuing mandates that would influence citizens that previously considered themselves free. Across the United States, businesses closed, airlines stopped flying, traffic stopped. Dr. Anthony Fauci became a household name, pressuring people into wearing masks, washing our hands for 20-second intervals, and social distancing away from other people.

Cultural wars started to break out. Before then, no one had ever heard of social distancing.

Despite those government mandates, the Federal Bureau of Prisons continued receiving people—seemingly immune from the admonitions of crowding large groups of people into confined spaces. We all have our jobs to do, and the people who worked in prisons had to do theirs. When administrators sent my notice to report, I complied with the orders I received.

Global pandemic notwithstanding, the morning for my surrender came in May 2020.

SELLING: HARD LESSONS LEARNED
Alec Burlakoff/ Training@aburlakoff.com

Before leaving the house to begin my transformation from family man to prisoner, I held my two daughters closely and told them I loved them. They both cried hysterically while my wife and I left them behind to walk toward our car. Life would change, and I would have to change with it.

As I look back upon those days, I'm reminded me of a story I heard from a sales trainer. He asked the audience a question:

- "When is the best time to plant an oak tree?"

People in the audience guessed at various answers. Some suggested it would be best to plant seeds in the winter, others guessed the fall. The trainer listened patiently before giving his response. "The best time to plant an oak tree was 20 years ago," he said. "The second-best time is today."

While walking away from my beautiful baby girls, the pain that I had caused became even more clear to me. I wasn't being separated from them because I pleaded guilty to a specific crime. By living without a disciplined, values-based code of conduct, I planted bad seeds at the start of my career. Over 20 years, those seeds didn't produce an oak tree. Instead, they produced the tree of poisonous fruit. I felt ashamed of the crimes I committed. It

SELLING: HARD LESSONS LEARNED
Alec Burlakoff/ Training@aburlakoff.com

all began 20 years previously, when I morphed from being a teacher into being a salesman that would do anything to close a deal.

Going to prison would open an opportunity for me to plant new seeds. To continue the oak tree analogy, I would have to plant seeds that would lead to something better—but first I had to fully understand the past. Shastry invited me to become the sales leader at Ingrid because of my response to his question about how I would induce physicians to write more prescriptions. I'd done it before and I told him that I could do it again. I told him what he wanted to hear, and in that moment, I became complicitous in a scheme that would serve interests. Unfortunately, my agreement to promote that plan brought disastrous consequences.

I looked back as I got into the car. That vision of my daughters hugging each other and crying made an indelible impression upon me. It solidified my commitment to sowing new seeds that would take me through the next 20 years. Instead of putting my company and career first, I would live by a different set of values going forward. I would sow seeds to grow an oak tree. To grow something strong, I would have to do more than plant a seed and wait. I would have to nurture those seeds. The science of botany tells us that one of the best ways to nurture those seeds is to spread manure over the ground. The manure feeds the seeds, helping them grow roots, then they grow through the manure to become stronger.

I prepared myself to grow through the manure of a 26-month prison term and made a personal commitment to emerge stronger.

Stephanie and I drove south to Miami, stopping for breakfast along the way. As I savored each bite of eggs and pancakes, I realized the luxury of liberty that I had taken for granted so many times before. On the one hand, I wanted to stop the clock from ticking so that I could enjoy more minutes with Stephanie. On the other, I wanted to get into the prison and get through the challenges I would have to endure. Before life would bring any more joy, I had to cross through the great unknown.

What would prison bring?

I got my answer after I stepped out of the car and started walking toward the prison's gates. Two guards approached to scold me for not wearing a mask. When I told them that I could return to the car to get a mask, they put me in my place.

"Stay right where you are," they ordered. "Your wife can go get your mask."

They didn't only want to tell me what to do, but also my wife. That moment crystalized how powerless I'd become.

Receiving orders would become a routine part of my life. Their demand made me feel as if I'd regressed to childhood, with my father yelling at me. A few years previously I considered myself at the top of my game. Yet the bad decisions I'd made along the way sunk me to the lowest point of my life.

After Stephanie returned from the car with my mask, the guards told her to get off the prison's property. They took me into custody, going through all the motions of fingerprinting, searching, mug shots, and processing me into a quarantine unit.

"Can you fight?" one of the guards asked, taunting me.

I told him that I could hold my own while in high school. Trying to be respectful, I followed up by saying that I've been trying to avoid fights since childhood.

"Yeah," he said, "you should try that. But you'll be better off if you remember that you know how to fight."

The guard led me into a dungeon-like environment, walked me down a series of pathways that felt like a maze of highly polished concrete and steel. I heard other people yelling from locked cells. He unlocked one of the steel doors and ordered me to step inside, telling me I'd be locked in quarantine for three weeks.

As a person who'd built a multi-decade career developing relationships with others, I'm not ashamed to admit that the solitude hurt me mentally. I'm ashamed of the crimes that I committed, and the way that I disappointed so many people, including myself. But I'm not ashamed to say that from the first moments, I could feel the prison experience crushing my spirit.

Although the guards told me that I'd stay in quarantine for three weeks, from people in adjacent cells I heard that it could be longer, depending upon whether anyone tested positive for COVID.

I wasn't allowed to bring anything with me into the barren cell. Part of serving time, I learned, meant that I'd have to accept a new reality. I couldn't get a toothbrush, mirror, razor, or even a cup to drink water. Most of the time, the guards kept the cell dark and cold. They'd pass meals through a slot in the door. Since I didn't have a clock, and I couldn't tell whether it was day or night, each breakfast became my marker for passing time.

After 21 breakfasts, the guards made my day by telling me to move out. I'd grown through one layer of manure and into the next. The guards escorted me from the solitary housing unit to the minimum-security camp. It was still prison, but compared to where I'd been, the camp felt like liberty.

By the time guards led me into the general population, my tolerance increased for the mental anguish of confinement. I could withstand the pains better because I saw others that had acclimated well. A counselor assigned me odd jobs, cleaning showers, mopping floors, or working in the kitchen.

After about two weeks, privileges opened, with limited access to the telephone and an email system. The prison didn't offer weights to exercise, but some of the other prisoners taught me how to jerry-rig a broom stick to use as barbell. We filled garbage bags with water, then tied the bags to each end of the broomstick to build strength. Since I couldn't concentrate on reading, I exercised every day. The physical exertion helped to block the tormenting thoughts. When not exercising, I used my radio to tune in to talk and sports shows as a distraction.

Within a few months, I could sense the gravity of loss from the problems I created. More manure to grow through. My wife of more than 20 years decided to move on without me. We remained cordial. I had to accept responsibility for the irreparable harm to our relationship my crimes had caused. As the weeks turned into months, I began putting a plan together on how I could recalibrate and rebuild upon my release.

With help from my mom, I got leads on a few potential jobs. They would not be anything glamorous, and they wouldn't come with the base salary that my previous jobs offered. Every day, I would have to prove myself. If I didn't bring value by generating sales, I would not be earning a paycheck. That didn't matter.

SELLING: HARD LESSONS LEARNED
Alec Burlakoff/ Training@aburlakoff.com

By losing everything that I held dear, I knew that I had hit bottom. The time had come to begin climbing. Once my mom gave me the contact information for potential jobs, I followed up with letter after letter.

With a felony conviction, I anticipated problems. They would simply become another layer I would have to grow through. To grow stronger, I had to work harder than ever to recalibrate. I made that 100% commitment to stabilize my life—this time, it wouldn't be about being the highest earner in the company. I wanted more balance, and I intended to work toward a position that would allow me to grow so that I could build stability that others took for granted.

After 10 months in the prison camp, I inquired with my case manager about my release plan. She surprised me, saying that I would go back into quarantine within a few days; the warden had agreed to transfer me to a community-based confinement program. Since the Bureau's risk-analysis tools indicated that I was at minimal risk of reoffending, administrators agreed that I was a good candidate to serve the remaining months of my sentence in a halfway house.

In the halfway house, I went through a few days of orientation before the case manager started pushing me out to find employment. Before getting there, I'd sown seeds that led to four interviews. Two car dealers wanted to meet with me, a recruiter in the solar industry had opportunities, and a company that brokered transactions for movers agreed to meet with me.

Each of those interviews concluded with a job offer. And why wouldn't they? The employers understood that I was a felon, but they could also test me without much risk on their part. The commission-only offer meant that the employers wouldn't have to pay me a penny unless I brought in sales first.

In each job interview, I responded to questions honestly. When the interviewers inquired if I had questions, I only had one:

- "What does the top-guy earn?"

Each of them told me the top-guy could earn about $250,000, but the average sales guy would earn about $80,000.

I've never been average, and I never would be. But I also understood that I wasn't going to commit the 100% effort necessary to be the top earner. The old Alec only thought about earning the highest commissions possible. It's what led me down that slippery slope that caused me to lose everything, including my reputation. The closer I advanced to 50, the more I knew that there would be more to

SELLING: HARD LESSONS LEARNED
Alec Burlakoff/ Training@aburlakoff.com

life than being the top salesperson on the team. I wanted to nurture relationships with my daughters and find a companion with whom I could share and build.

After losing so much, I wanted a higher quality of life more than I wanted to become the highest earning salesman on anyone's team. I didn't have any interest in working the 24/7 schedule that dominated my career for the past 20 years. Yet knowing what I knew about qualifying leads, nurturing relationships, and using my 98/2 principle, I felt confident that I could balance out the quality of life I wanted, while still being in the top three earners of any sales team.

Both my dad and my brother had built great careers in the car business, but that wasn't what I wanted. The opportunity with the solar company sounded promising, but I quickly surmised that it would take several months to build a pipeline that would lead to any commissions. By process of elimination, I chose to start with telemarketing sales for the moving company—the least glamours of the three.

The moving company operated out of a few thousand square feet in a strip mall. Rather than investing in trucks and dollies and straps and blankets that were necessary for the moving trade, the company filled its space with a grid of cheap desks, cubicles, basic computer screens, and telephones.

SELLING: HARD LESSONS LEARNED
Alec Burlakoff/ Training@aburlakoff.com

Scores of people sat in those cubicles day after day responding to leads that would come in.

The sales manager told me that I'd receive a script and begin talking to prospective customers. If I took the job, I could control my own destiny by earning commissions from every sale.

This was a layer of manure that I didn't anticipate. While looking over the grid of cubicles, I thought back to the old days of wearing designer suits and entertaining clients with unlimited expense accounts. But I also considered what that life had gotten me—a trip to federal prison. This new position would put me at the bottom. No one would care about my previous responsibilities, or my felony background. If I could convert prospective moving clients into paying customers, I could climb another level toward stability. I may require a willingness to pass through a few years of manure, but in time, if I nurtured the seeds well, I anticipated that I could grow from disgrace into a man of character, perhaps with the strength of an oak tree.

CONCLUSION:

In the summer of 2022, more than two years have passed since I transitioned from prison to the halfway house. After completing my obligation to the Bureau of Prisons, I began working my way through a new set of challenges, completing the requirements of Supervised Release. The crime I committed brought sanctions that include an obligation to pay tens of millions in restitution.

Commitment helped me to reach my goal of being included in the top-three earners at the moving company, allowing me to contribute several thousand dollars each month toward my restitution, while also doing my part to contribute child support/alimony payments. I've grown from living hand-to-mouth. More importantly, I've begun sowing seeds to make a more positive impact on the lives of others. I'm particularly eager to work with universities and businesses who seek training for future sales leaders—speaking honestly about the costs of planting seeds that can lead to a poisonous tree.

I'll encourage people to sow seeds for oak trees instead. They're 20 years in the making.

Each reader that invested the time to make it through this story will determine whether any takeaways exist. I'll leave with 10 simple lessons that I'll call the Burlakoff Success Principles:

DEFINE YOUR SUCCESS:

At the start of a career, each person should define success. If a person knows what he's striving to achieve, the person will be in a better position to understand the opportunity costs that come with every decision. The lessons I've learned convince me that it's better to work toward a higher quality of life than to strive for higher sales at all costs.

- How do you define success?

SET GOALS THAT ALIGN WITH YOUR DEFINITION OF SUCCESS:

If you define what you want, you can chart a course of incremental steps. Those steps should bridge the gap, getting you to where you want to be—without compromising your integrity. Hard lessons taught me to reject opportunities to earn more income because they would disrupt the life balance I wanted to cultivate. Instead, I set goals that allow me to meet financial obligations. I took the incremental step of working in a grimy sales position, but do so with my dignity intact, knowing that it's another step toward what I want to become. I'm growing through the manure that will lead me to strength.

- What goals are you setting, and how to do they align with your definition of success?

MAKE YOUR COMMITMENT:

To succeed at anything, a person must commit. Before I learned the hard lessons that led to my imprisonment, I made the commitment of doing anything to get that sale. Now, I make a commitment to life-balance. I may not earn as much in commissions, but I'll stay the course of living in accordance with how I define success.

- In what ways do your commitments align with how you define success?

VISUALIZE YOUR SUCCESS:

When starting out, don't focus on the challenges. Visualize how you can become the best that you want to become, consistent with how you define success. Then see yourself in that role. This exercise helped me get through the challenges of incremental steps, like saying goodbye to my family when going into prison or accepting a commission-only job in telemarketing. Instead of seeing the challenges, I saw how the incremental step could advance me on the path to what I wanted to become.

- In what ways are the decisions you're making today going to lead to the person you want to become?

TAKE ACTION:

Take the necessary action steps to go from one challenge to the next. Each step will open new opportunities that wouldn't have existed before. Make sure that each step aligns with success, as you define it. This exercise led to the completion of my manuscript. The manuscript becomes a tool that I'll use to make an impact on the lives of others.

- How did your action steps last week open opportunities for higher levels of success this week?

CREATE ACCOUNTABILITY TOOLS:

A wise leader wrote, "if you can't measure the progress, it doesn't exist." As a sales leader, we always look to results. Sometimes, we fail to look at the tiny steps we should take to get the results we want. Measure everything and use those measurements to refine your strategy. Every day, align your strategy with the way in which you define success.

- In what ways are you tracking the micro steps that will lead to your success, as you define success?

SELLING: HARD LESSONS LEARNED
Alec Burlakoff/ Training@aburlakoff.com

STAY AWARE:

Every decision we make comes with opportunity costs. Think about those decisions and assess whether the decisions will advance you in the short term, and in the long term. Your commitment to success will make others aware of you, and in time, opportunities will open. Despite working in telemarketing sales, I'm grateful for opportunities to work with universities, businesses, and the media to share lessons I learned from a lifetime in sales.

- What efforts are you making to track opportunities in your industry, and to make others aware of you?

CELEBRATE ACHIEVEMENTS:

Track the relationship between micro success and macro-opportunities. It takes ten pennies to make a dime, and ten dimes to make a dollar. Never scoff at the little victories because they can lead to something better. Rather than missing my days as a high-rolling VP of sales for a billion-dollar company, I celebrate each opportunity to sit a small desk and work through the prospective leads that come to me—knowing that by following the 98/2 rule, I'll always exceed expectations.

- What tiny achievements led to your greatest success?

EXPRESS APPRECIATION:

By living in a state of gratitude, we empower ourselves and we strengthen our communities. In sales, some people envy the successes that others are making. That envy can lead to bad decisions, such as the decisions that led to imprisonment for me. Instead, always recognize the relationship between daily decisions and prospects for success—as we define success.

- How have others responded when you show your appreciation for the ways they're influencing your prospects for success?

After decades of selling, those are some of the hard lessons I've learned.

Made in the USA
Las Vegas, NV
10 January 2023

65387495R00134